Communication Skills Training

2 in 1

How To Handle Difficult Conversations, Improve Your Persuasion Skills, And Become A Master At Public Speaking

SHIRLEY COLE

Copyright 2019 © Shirley Cole
All rights reserved.

No part of this guide may be reproduced in any form without permission in writing from the publisher except in the case of review.

Legal & Disclaimer

The following document is reproduced below with the goal of providing information that is as accurate and reliable as possible.

This declaration is deemed fair and valid by both the American Bar Association and the Committee of Publishers Association and is legally binding throughout the United States.

Furthermore, the transmission, duplication or reproduction of any of the following work including specific information will be considered an illegal act irrespective of if it is done electronically or in print. This extends to creating a secondary or tertiary copy of the work or a recorded copy and is only allowed with an express written consent from the Publisher. All additional right reserved.

The information in the following pages is broadly considered to be a truthful and accurate account of facts, and as such any inattention, use or misuse of the information in question by the reader will render any resulting actions solely under their purview. There are no scenarios in which the publisher or the original author of this work can be in any fashion deemed liable for any hardship or damages that may befall them after undertaking information described herein.

Additionally, the information in the following pages is intended only for informational purposes and should thus be thought of as universal. As befitting its nature, it is presented without assurance regarding its prolonged validity or interim quality. Trademarks that are mentioned are done without written consent and can in no way be considered an endorsement from the trademark holder.

Table of Contents

Book 1: Communication In Relationships 7
Introduction 8
Chapter One: Positive Communication 18
Chapter Two: Relationships At Work 63
Chapter Three: Managing Conflict 79
Chapter Four: Becoming A Better Listener 110
Chapter Five: Trust, Honesty, And Respect............ 154
Chapter Six: Relationship Killers............................. 183
Chapter Seven: Ending Relationships 207
Final Words 216
Book 2: Communication In The Workplace 222
Introduction 223
Chapter One: The Incredible Power of Effective Communication in The Workplace 231
Chapter Two: How to Develop Effective and Persuasive Communication Skills at Work.............. 262
Chapter Three: How to Effectively Handle Difficult Situations and People in the Workplace................... 335
Chapter Four: How to Be The Most Effective Leader You Can Be 367

Chapter Five: The Most Common Communication Mistakes and How to Avoid Them 394

Chapter Six: Expert Tips and Tricks for Effective Communication in The Workplace 402

Bonus Chapter: How to Become a Master at Public Speaking 413

Final Words 422

Book 1: Communication In Relationships

How To Build And Maintain Bonds With People In Life, Love, And The Workplace

Introduction

There are few things more difficult and frustrating than relationships. Romantic or otherwise, navigating the interpersonal bonds that make up our social networks can be a stressful and confusing process. Romantic relationships, though, are especially trying. When two people are committed to being together, they have to work through issues that might on some level make them want to just give up. What many people fail to realize is just how much hard work is really required to make a relationship successful and to allow both halves of the whole to flourish, both together and individually; to achieve all of their dreams both independently and as a team. When two people are in a committed long-term relationship, there is a sort of symbiosis that occurs. While both individuals are distinctly separate, they also come together and create something new and unique, something far greater than the sum of its parts. Think of a long term relationship between two people like a project they are co-creators of. They form an incredibly intimate bond together and get to know each other to such a deep and thorough extent that no one else knows either of them better than they know each other. The reason why a relationship is such a complex and confusing enterprise is a direct result of this bond. Whatever happens to one partner deeply affects the other, whether they want it to or not. Everything that happens to each of them becomes the direct business and problem of the other. In order for both parties to be happy and fulfilled under these circumstances, a great deal of communication and teamwork is required.

Both of these skills are difficult to practice even at the best of times when everything is smooth and rosy and the relationship is ticking over nicely. When times get hard, however, our ability to put these skills into practice is really put to the test. There's a good reason why between forty and fifty percent of marriages end in divorce. Nothing lasts in this world and making a relationship really go the distance is an incredibly hard thing to do. A lifetime is a long time, and it's a very long time to put up with all the inevitably annoying and troubling aspects of our partner's character, no matter how much we love them. Relationships don't usually break down due to a lack of love. If love was all that was needed to make things work, the divorce rate would be much lower than it is. Relationships can fall apart for any number of reasons, but the causes almost always stem from the same root problem: a lack of good communication.

Every relationship faces problems, and every couple will be tested. A good, strong relationship isn't about being perfect or keeping a squeaky clean record. It's about rising to every challenge and overcoming all the obstacles you face. It's about being able to admit when you're wrong and making a genuine effort to try to make things better. It's about not giving up, no matter what, and having each other's backs until the end. A strong relationship is one based on teamwork, not competition. It's one that approaches problems with a mentality of 'how do we handle this together?' and then looking for solutions, rather than blaming each other and dwelling on the problems themselves. It's not you versus them, it's the two of you versus the issue, every time.

Many couples find it very difficult to properly communicate with each other. They struggle to find the right words to say or the right state of mind to properly connect at the same time. This lack of communication leads to arguments and fights which only make the problem worse, allowing emotions to spiral out of control and feelings to get hurt. It's common for two people who love each other more than anything to lay awake at night crying, one in their bed and the other on the couch, each wishing their partner could see things the way they do. Many relationships are characterized not by mutual support but by petty fights and bickering that never seem to end. Couples fail to listen to each other or approach problem's together, instead preferring to focus on who's to blame or who's done something to hurt the other. Instead of showing love and affection to one another, there is more often than not an atmosphere of tension and resentment. All of these issues ultimately boil down to a lack of effective, calm, empathetic, loving communication.

When a relationship is based around a mutual bond of trust and openness that facilitates this type of vitally important communication, it's much harder for problems to take root and grow in the same way that they do in relationships that lack it. The majority of issues that arise throughout the course of a relationship can be worked out just through sitting down and calmly discussing them from both people's points of view, no matter how long it might take or how many times you might have to say something to get your point across. Communication is a skill, and like any skill, it takes a lot of practice to get good at it. No matter the difficulties that you and your partner face, you can both learn how to communicate in a way that allows you to overcome them. Whether you feel like you're not being heard, or your partner thinks that you don't understand them, or you just want to be able to have a conversation about your problems without it descending into fighting or yelling, this book contains the information you need to break new ground and move your relationship with each other to the next level.

This book will provide you with the tools you need to begin communicating well and improve your relationships in every aspect of your life. Although it focuses primarily on relationships of the romantic kind, it also discusses navigating more platonic relationships at length, and many of the lessons that can be learned from romantic relationships can be applied elsewhere in your life. I wrote this book by drawing from the lessons I've learned from years of studying relationships and helping couples to cooperate.

Over the course of my career as a professional family therapist, since I started back in 2004, I've coached hundreds of people on moving through difficulties they faced in their lives and relationships. I love to help people, and being able to assist others in getting through the tough situations we all face is an incredibly fulfilling experience for me. It was this passion and drive that inspired to collect my thoughts and lessons into this book as a way to spread the knowledge I have to as wide an audience as possible. It will deliver simple, practical, proven techniques for improving relationships — that's any relationship with anyone in your life, not just with your partner. With the advice this book contains, you'll learn how to think, talk, and act in order to repair holes in your relationships and resolve or prevent arguments so that you can provide your loved ones with the support they deserve. The things we'll be talking about over the course of the next few chapters will revolutionize the way you treat the people that you care about most in life, ensuring it's your one-stop-guide to improving your relationships, maintaining a loving, lasting bond with your partner, and preventing issues from tearing you apart from the things that matter the most to you.

Couples who can communicate effectively are more likely to have a happy, fulfilling, lasting relationship than those who can't. Communicating well allows you to pick up on when something is wrong so that you can nip it in the bud by addressing it before it has the chance to grow into a larger and further reaching problem. When you can sit down and properly talk about the issues you face with your partner, with the freedom for each of you to be heard and allowed the time and space to properly make your case, you can sort problems out before they have a chance to fester and cause deep resentment and emotional scars. My clients, old and new, tell me on a regular basis that the things I've taught them have helped them to change their lives and put themselves and their relationships on the right path. If you were to go to couples therapy with me, I'd be telling you the exact same things that I outline in this book; overcoming the obstacles that any relationship faces about being able to give each other the chance to express how you feel about every aspect of the problems you face. It's only when we adopt this attitude of openness, patience, and understanding that we feel like we can be heard, enlightened as to how our partner feels, and able to put problems in the past while learning from our mistakes and going forward together.

No matter how much you might love your partner, you can't read their mind. You need to give them the opportunity to tell you how they really feel, and you need to be able to accept whatever they say, regardless of your own private feelings about it. Their feelings matter, and if you can't or won't validate the way they feel they'll only grow to resent you in the long run. This book is a promise; it's a promise to you that you have what it takes to fix your relationship. With the help of this book, you *will* see a tangible difference in the way you and your partner work together. You *will* learn how to make your relationship happy, lasting, and loving, and you *will* become wiser, more emotionally intelligent person. Without learning the lessons that this book contains, how might your relationship play out in the long run? How long do you think you can make things last if you don't fully understand and appreciate the basic building blocks necessary to actually get into the trenches and do the heavy lifting? Will you be able to come to solutions on problems and move on for good without half-solved issues coming back to haunt you in the future? Every second you delay is a second of the time you have with your partner that ticks away, frustrated and confused when it could and should be calm and loving. Don't wait. Change your relationship now! Change your life, change your happiness, and gain the skills you need to in order to make your relationship last and create a lifetime of happy and fulfilling memories that you can share with the people closest to you.

Chapter One: Positive Communication

In this chapter, you'll learn how to communicate in a positive and productive manner. Before we can go into the best ways to communicate, it's important to understand the gulf in processing and understanding communication that exists between men and women.

Differences in Male and Female Communication

Communication is a highly relative concept. All of us communicate slightly differently, in our own individual ways, much like everybody's fingerprints seem similar at a glance, but each person is unique. In addition to this, we can also identify differing trends in how men and women communicate. Men tend to rely more on logic and reasoning in order to communicate and relate.

They see things more mechanically, with an emphasis on problem-solving and wanting to fix things. When they encounter a situation they need to overcome, men are more likely to want to break it down and work out how to solve any problems in order to address the issue as it is and then move on. Women, however, tend to be more emotionally focused. They are more likely to use relational examples in order to communicate their thoughts and rely on talking about their problems in order to work out how they feel and then work through and fix their problems on their own and in their own time, rather than forcing a solution straight away. Women, therefore, feel a desire to be heard and validated by their partners, whereas men often feel discussing the emotional side of things is unnecessary as long as they solve the root problem.

This difference in communication can lead to a great deal of difficulty when problems arise in relationships. Women are often frustrated by their partner's single-minded focus on solving the problem and sweeping everything else under the mat when all they want is to feel heard, understood, and loved. Men are better off being patient and listening attentively to their female partners while they describe how and why a certain situation or sequence of events has made them feel a certain way, giving them time to explain exactly how they feel. Another point I want to make clear here is that women often don't make this plain to their male partners — they will talk about how they feel and use examples, then expect their partner to read between the lines and understand what they're getting at rather than clearly stating that they simply need to be heard and understood, regardless of whether the problem is solved yet or not.

When men and women fail to speak each other's language, neither side is getting what they need. This leads to a whole host of totally unnecessary problems; confusion, the frustration that in turn leads to annoyance and anger, bitterness, resentment, and often, drama. Once bad feelings are involved and the gloves come off, situations can quickly get out of hand for no reason. All that was ever needed was a mutual understanding that men and women tend to process situations and communicate in different ways. When a couple has that understanding, it's much easier to prevent any issues from boiling over.

Another issue that biological differences in communication can lead to is differing assumptions and expectations about how an event or interaction should occur. Women and men tend to have different needs and priorities, as well as different interpretations of the same experience. This can lead to miscommunication where one person expects one thing but the other has a completely different set of assumptions, even though they've both had the same experience. Men and women tend to interpret the same things in different ways, owing to our different biological makeups. As a result of millions of years of hominid evolution, men are wired to be problem solvers. To the typical man, communication serves a couple of clear purposes. Either there's a statement that needs to be made or a problem that needs to be solved. Women, however, usually have a less limited view of communication. To them, talking isn't just a means to an end, but an end in and of itself. Women tend to want to talk about their problems because it's a way to work out how they feel and order their thoughts. They don't necessarily expect or want the person they're talking to try to fix things; they just want to get it off their chest. In fact, just talking about things can often make women feel like a burden has been lessened. Women communicate to strengthen their bond with their partner and promote intimacy and closeness. Through sharing their thoughts, they release their negative feelings. For them, communication with their partner is about having a supportive and non-judgemental arena in which they can express themselves openly.

This simple difference in the way communication tends to be perceived between the sexes can lead to a whole host of small problems and irritations in a relationship, all of which add up and can snowball into something far bigger if not rectified or kept in check. A good example of this is when a stressed out wife phones her husband and tells him that she's having a bad day at work and then becomes annoyed when later that evening he doesn't even ask her about it. To the woman, her mentioning her bad day on the phone to her husband earlier was a clue or prompt for him to ask her about it later on. She thought that by hinting about her bad day, her husband would naturally ask her about it, because he's her husband and he loves and cares about her, so he knows she'd want to open up and tell him all about it. However, in the husband's mind, things look very different. It's not that his wife mentioned she had a bad day completely passed him by, but that he has a different approach to dealing with the problems he faces and assumes that what seems to work for him will work for his wife. He takes his wife's comment at face value, as a statement that she's had a bad day — not realizing that she wants to talk about it. Whereas women tend to want to talk about their problems in order to work through them, men are much more likely to simply want to forget about them and move on if there's nothing more they can do. The husband had therefore assumed that his wife would rather not relive her bad day with him by bringing it all back up and talking about it, so instead he works to distract and comfort her rather than giving her what she needs.

This tendency to distract from and try to forget about problems is a real problem for some men. It is common for them to self-medicate with alcohol and other drugs, both legal and illegal. While women are not immune to this either, it is especially common with men, who aren't used to accepting or dealing with their emotions for fear of being stigmatized and outcast or labeled as weak. Many men have no one to talk to about their difficult and often conflicting feelings, which can make their lives incredibly lonely even when they're surrounded by friends and family. Women should try to be there for their husbands and boyfriends, in order to give them an outlet for their emotions and help them to process and understand them. However, keep in mind that attempting to comfort men when they're feeling upset and hurt can easily backfire and make them withdraw even more; they'd sometimes rather forget about their problems than confront them at all. Persuasion from their partner to tackle these issues can provoke a defensive reaction in men. Until a man is ready to deal with whatever issues they're facing, questions and encouragement can do more harm than good. It's a good idea for women to remind their male partners that they're there for them whenever they want or need to talk, and then allow them to come to them in their own time when they're ready.

Men typically keep their problems to themselves and don't see the need to open up or share, whereas women are more likely to talk to other women when they have a problem they need to deal with or they need to make a decision. This is because, on the whole, men relate to other men based on the power dynamic and dominance status between them, while women tend to be more relationship oriented and look for connections and ways to relate to one another through common ground and shared experience. Women focus on building a rapport with one another by asking questions, whereas men usually prefer to give information rather than asking questions. They instead share experiences as a way of competing, which often leads to instances of one-upmanship. However, men can have a serious disagreement and even come to blows over it and then move on and forget all about it, whereas women are often more emotionally committed to a sense of being right or wrong and can hold grudges for far longer. Women build relationships in order to get things done, whereas men build relationships by working together to get things done. Making communication work in a male and female couple involves not criticizing the way the other sex communicates, but rather learning how to adapt and work together despite the natural differences we share.

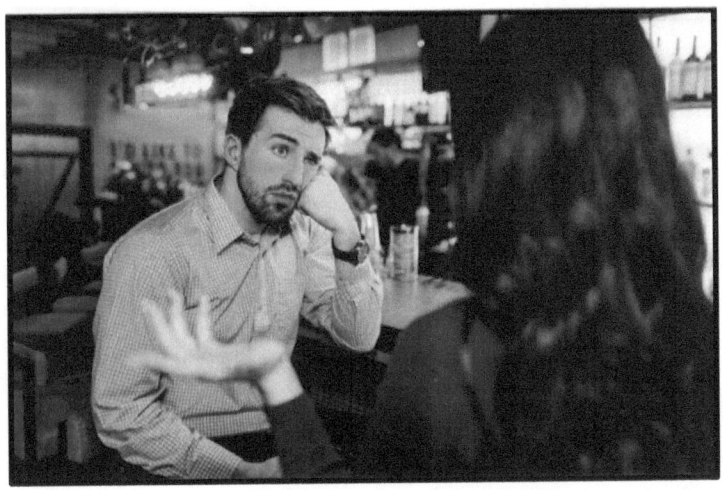

When men are upset, they tend to keep their thoughts to themselves rather than confiding in anyone. This can be because they struggle to communicate their problems, as they haven't verbalized them even to themselves. They're also taught from a young age to bottle up their emotions and swallow their feelings rather than expressing themselves. They're told consistently and frequently that crying is for women that they should instead 'man up' and just deal with the problems they face alone. Expressing emotions or crying is widely seen as being a sign of weakness by a large portion of men. Women, however, have no such social restrictions on them and are far more used to expressing themselves and shedding tears without shame.

The problem-solving nature of men commonly proves frustrating and annoying to their female partners even when they do take the time to listen to what their partner is saying. They tend to be looking to problem solve naturally, without even thinking about it. Listening patiently is hard for men because they have to fight the urge to interrupt and problem solve. When they see an opportunity to give advice or help or they see what they think is a solution to the problem, they will often interrupt the conversation to offer their thoughts and try to 'fix' whatever problem their partner has. The problem with this, of course, is that more often than not their partner isn't looking to have their problem solved. In all likeliness, there isn't really a problem, and they already know what course of action they're going to take in response to something. They're not looking for a fix, they're trying to vent. They want to talk just to be heard and understood, something that is an alien concept to many men. Receiving unsolicited (and often ill-informed) advice from interrupting boyfriends and husbands is an infuriatingly common occurrence for women, often leading to anger and resentment. It's made more annoying by the fact that if they just waited to hear their partners out, men would find that they don't actually need a solution, anyway; instead, they tend to jump in at the first chance as soon as they think they might have even a fraction of a good idea to help their partners. Their intentions are well placed, but fall hopelessly far from the mark.

When you're faced with misunderstandings as a result of miscommunication in your relationship, it's a good idea to be as explicit and clear as possible going forwards in order to avoid making the same mistakes again. A great line for men who seem to always get it wrong is to ask 'Do you want my opinion, or do you want me to listen?'. This might seem blunt, but if it avoids them being unable to satisfy their partner's needs properly, it's an effective and useful tool. This bluntness is the key to cutting through any beating around the bush or treading on tiptoes that might be occurring in your relationship. Women should tell men exactly what they need to feel understood and loved. Men need explicit and clear instructions that they can stick to and work to perfect. Logical steps laid out for them in an easily understandable way will help them to learn what it is their partner needs. Leaving them to work things out for themselves through subtle hints will only make this harder and waste both people's time and energy feeling upset and frustrated at the relationship. It's unfair to expect men to work these things out when they usually lack the emotional knowledge necessary to do it;

both halves of the couple should be clear about what they want and need from each other so that the majority of misunderstandings and hurt feelings can be totally avoided.

As a result of the differences between male and female communication, some women are left feeling like their husbands or boyfriends don't care about them because they can't intuitively read them as well as they might like. They feel like their feelings have been disregarded or invalidated, and their needs go unresolved. While this is a problem, it isn't necessarily true that it's because their partners don't care about them. Men tend to be less emotionally intelligent than women. Men need prompting sometimes. They won't always pick up on things. That doesn't mean that they're not in love or committed to the relationship. In general, men want to make their partners happy. They want to be good, successful husbands and boyfriends — they just don't always understand how to do this until they're shown.

Women relying on assumptions that their hints will be recognized and understood will not only get them anywhere, but it will make things far harder for their partners. When women are annoyed by their men's ineptness at meeting their needs, the end result is their male partners feel rejected. They feel like they're the reason something went wrong like they can't properly fulfill or satisfy their women. They feel emasculated, inadequate, and hurt, all of which often manifest themselves in the form of anger. When a woman makes her man aware of her need to be heard and understood, the entire dynamic of the relationship can change, because the man has had it spelled out for him and knows what he has to do to make his woman feel loved and appreciated. There's no need for hurt, anger, or fights if both partners can clearly tell each other what they want and need. If a man can manage his response, listen and ask compassionate questions as a woman explores her thoughts, conflicts will subside quickly. In the same way, if a woman can learn to understand that her male partner isn't trying to be insensitive or hurtful, but simply needs help to meet her needs, things can be concluded in a positive and respectful manner, bringing both people closer together.

Another factor that plays into this is the way in which issues are brought up in a relationship. How you bring up issues determines the level of cooperation and understanding you'll receive from your partner. Wording, tone of voice, and context are all part of how something you say is interpreted by another person, and this effect is compounded when the things you're bringing up can provoke a defensive reaction in the person you're speaking to. If your partner feels like they're being criticized, they're going to be sensitive to what you say, even if you pick your words carefully and speak as softly and gently as possible. When people bring up issues in a negative way, however, with poorly chosen words or a hostile tone of voice, such as saying 'did you forget to ask me about my day?', the chances of them provoking a defensive reaction from their partner are much higher. It's therefore vitally important that when you raise any issues that you might have with your partner's behavior or attitude that you try to be as sensitive and careful as possible, in order to try to avoid your words having a negative connotation. If you don't, all you're doing is telling them that they're bad at being your partner and they're making you unhappy, which will likely only lead to issues spiraling out of control.

It's extremely common for men to feel like they're being tested by their wives or girlfriends to see if they pick up on hints, which is a frustrating thing for them to experience. Men tend to be relatively straightforward; they don't appreciate or have much time for mind games. They would much prefer their significant others to be clear about their meaning and intentions rather than saying something different to how they truly feel and relying on hints and assumptions to get their point across.

The fact that evolutionary biology influences how we think, how we act, and how we treat others means that our ability to have a civilized and measured perspective is constantly at battle with our nature and our primitive, biological urges and instincts. Learning how to communicate well with your partner means being able to take these evolutionary factors into account when considering any issue, problem, or circumstance where they might be at work behind the scenes, and they're active more often than they're not. For example, a lot of guys are extremely hesitant to ask for help, because their ego tells them that they need to be totally self-sufficient and able to handle everything on their own. They don't want to be looked at as inferior or less capable in some way, both by other men and by women. They're even less likely to ask for help when they're in the presence of women. Women, however, are often quick to ask for help when they're struggling with something because they don't feel anywhere near as much pressure to appear capable and independent. Women will often seek advice just for the sake of taking the chance to improve the situation at hand, regardless of whether or not it assists them in achieving their objective. When a woman approaches a man (especially in a workplace environment), the man is quite likely to automatically assume that the woman needs his help. They will also be relatively happy to help because it's an opportunity to demonstrate their capability and prowess to a woman. They might not be particularly patient, however, because they tend to view this as a favor to be potentially taken advantage of in the future, rather than seeing it as an opportunity just to help another person.

Additionally, men like to assert themselves when talking to women in order to show that they are confident and that they know what they're doing, the same reason they can be so hesitant to ask for help. They don't like being seen as weak. They can also be more likely to dismiss a woman's opinions for no other reason than the fact that they come from a woman, especially if it's on a topic they feel women shouldn't or couldn't know much about. Some men also find sustaining conversations that have long points difficult, especially when it's not something they want to be talking about in the first place. This is why when they're sent long texts, they often reply to the last couple of points mentioned, instead of the entire text.

> **Qick Tip:** These sex-based differences in communication are trends identifiable across broad populations of people across the world and are biological in origin. This doesn't mean that they're always accurate, however. Many men are very emotionally intelligent and innately understand that women need to talk to express themselves. I've also met many women that would prefer to problem solve rather than talk about the way they feel at all. There will always be individual differences, and I address these biological differences only to

> highlight the broad divisions in the way men and women process and understand communication.

Secrets Of Positive Communication

Communication is a form of art, and it needs to be practiced in order to be effective. In order for communication to take place, there must be at least two parties between whom a message can be transferred: the sender and the receiver. Noise can hinder this process — both physical noise, such as other people talking or music playing in the background, and mental noise, such as thoughts and feelings in the mind of the receiver that stop the message from coming through clearly and being fully understood — which can result in the receiver getting a very different message than the sender attempted to communicate. The goal of positive communication is therefore for a message to be transmitted clearly and with as little misunderstanding as possible on the part of the audience receiving it. Communicating positively is about ensuring this goal is met and that both sides understand the intent behind the message, as well as the message itself.

Here are five secrets of positive communication that will help you to become a master communicator:

1. Express to be understood - When you're the person doing the talking, keep in mind that your goal isn't to persuade or convince anyone or to change any minds. Your goal is to be understood, first and foremost, so speak in a way that accomplishes this aim before worrying about any other purposes of your communication.

2. Seek to understand, rather than agree - When you're the receiver, you have a goal, too. Your aim should be to understand what the sender is trying to communicate, rather than seeking to agree with whatever they're saying.

3. Use the language understood by the receiver - Speak in a way that is tailored to your audience. If you're speaking to a child, you should use words that reflect their reading and comprehension level and can be thoroughly understood by them. Likewise, if you're speaking to someone who is an expert in the field you're discussing, you'd use a more specific form of language with specialized words to make your point more clearly.

4. **Stay focused on your task** - Whatever your role is in the process of communication at a given time, you should aim to accomplish the goals of that role as well as possible. This means staying focused and grounding yourself totally in the present moment by paying attention to what is happening. If you're the sender, then stay focused on your audience — how they're feeling and whether or not they understand what you're saying. If you doubt that they've fully understood what you mean, then repeat yourself and try to explain your point in different words. If you're the receiver, you should also be paying close attention to what the sender is saying. Reflect back to them your understanding of what they've

said so that you can double check that you've gotten the true essence of the meaning they're attempting to transmit.

5. Maintain appropriate contact throughout communication - Keeping both parties focused on the act of communication means maintaining an appropriate level of personal contact that anchors them both in the act itself. This can be achieved through good eye contact, facial expressions, and affirmative body language and vocalizations from both people to indicate that they understand what each other are saying. Smiling can help a lot in this regard, as can being positive and saying 'yes'.

> **Quick tip:** You can use these secrets of communication to make sure that you express yourself well and listen intently to your partner in order to practice positive communication within your relationship, as well as making sure you're communicating effectively with other people in your life.

Body Language

Although we've historically used spoken language to do the bulk of our communicating, a large part of the expression is actually non-verbal; in fact, our body language can say more about our true thoughts, feelings, and intentions than the words we use or the way that we speak. This is why understanding our body language can help us to better understand others and forge deeper connections with our partners. When you better understand body language, you will be more able to express yourself and avoid miscommunication, something which can be extremely costly; it can make your relationships with others or your partner worse and stop you from achieving your goals.

When we're talking to someone face to face, we actually have three voices of communication that transmit messages to our audience. These are:

1. **The words that we say**
2. **Our tone of voice**
3. **Body language: our gestures, facial expressions, and eye contact**

Although you might think that the most important part of your communication when you're talking to someone is the words that you use, that aren't the case. In reality, the context of what we're saying is heavily influenced by our body language and tone of voice, and this is where the real meaning lies. We are wired to instinctively read and understand body language, even though we rarely notice that we're doing it.

What's more, if the words a person says don't match their tone of voice or their body language, we disregard what they say and trust what their body is telling us. When a person is sending mixed messages with their voices of communication, people pay attention to the words said only a fraction of the time. When someone's words are at odds with their actions, our gut instinct is to go with what their body is telling us. Body language is a largely automatic process. When we pay attention to it, we can control it through conscious effort, but as soon as we forget about it, it goes back to going an automatic process. This means that often when we're trying to lie or disguise our true feelings, our body language will betray us and give the other person the distinct impression that we're holding something back.

Interestingly, body language also varies between men and women, just like other forms of communication. Men usually don't give off many facial expressions in their day to day conversations and are more likely to avoid eye contact and fold their arms in order to maintain a defensive stance when talking. They will nod to show their agreement with something that has been said. Women, on the other hand, are more likely to hold eye contact during face to face conversations. They tend to be more comfortable with physical proximity and will smile and laugh more than men, as well as using their hands to express themselves. Unlike men, women nod to show that they are listening and understand what is being communicated to them, not that they necessarily agree with it. These differences are likely to be because of the different evolutionary pressures that men and women have faced throughout history. Men are far more likely to be involved in a violent struggle with each other than women, so they tend to be less open and more naturally defensive, especially when they're speaking to other men that they don't know well. Eye contact between men is also more likely to be taken as an aggressive gesture than it is between women or between men and women.

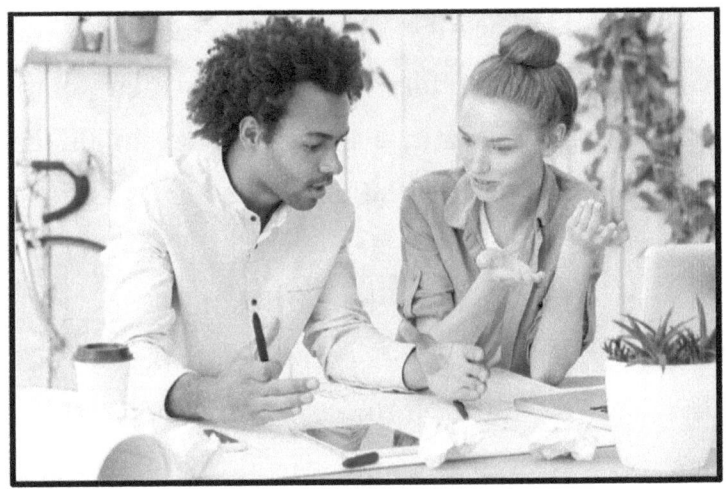

Positive Body Language

When you're learning how to communicate positively, it's important to take the highly influential role of body language into account. Notice how if you give someone a compliment, they will be likely to extend their arm away from their body and towards you, as though they are symbolically trying to push it away. This subconscious action stems from the expectation that our society has programmed into us that we're not supposed to accept compliments readily in order to seem modest and to avoid coming across as arrogant. The person receiving the compliment therefore often uses their body language to reject it, even while they might be thanking you for it with their words.

If you want to forge better relationships with others, you need to work on reflecting better body language to them. Not only will this make them feel better about their interaction with you and feel happier in themselves as a direct result, but it will also make you feel better about yourself and your interaction with that person. This increased positivity in both people can lead to a more fulfilling and smoothly running relationship between the two of you, regardless of what capacity you know them in. When people are giving off positive body language, it's a sign that they feel happy in their own skin and are confident in themselves. This aura of positivity instinctively makes others like and trusts that person more, directly improving the relationship they share.

In order to improve your body language and communicate positively with all of your body, follow these steps:

- **Accept compliments into your chest** - Rather than pushing away with your arms when you receive a compliment, instead try to place your hand on your chest to symbolize accepting it and taking it to heart. This will both make yourself feel better and make the person you're talking to feel happier and at ease in your company.

- **Hold your head up high** - Push your chin up to just above level, so that your head is very slightly tilted back. This will serve to elevate your head and help you express a confident and engaging air.

- **Push your shoulders back** - This pushes out your chest and straightens your back, causing you to walk, stand, or sit more upright. This confident posture sends out the right message to the people you talk to.

- **Open up your body** - Avoid crossing your arms or holding your hands in front of you. Doing this forms a 'gate' that makes you seem defensive, unsure, and closed off from interaction with others. Think of it like a natural barrier that you unconsciously create when you reject the reality of the outside world. It shows that you feel weaker than and inferior to others. If you hold your hands at your sides you will seem more relaxed, open, and inviting, bringing you better relationships and more opportunities.

A strange and interesting phenomenon is that improving your own body language in this way actually makes you feel more confident and capable. The very act of having the body language of a confident and self-assured person makes it a reality. You begin to radiate whole different energy from your being, giving off better signals to the people around you. In this way, making yourself more open and approachable to others improves your relationship with them. People that are less confident and don't want to interact with other people tend to have poorer relationships than those that do. When you begin to consciously use more positive body language, you will, therefore, improve the relationships you have with the people around you.

These improvements will benefit not only the relationships you have with your friends, family, and coworkers but also the one you have with your partner. You will find that giving off the right subconscious signals to each other by using more positive body language brings the two of you closer together, and cultivates a stronger and more intimate bond. When you're giving off the wrong body language, your partner picks up on it, consciously or not. They're affected by these negative signals and feel more distant from you as a result. If you can work to improve your body language, then not only will you feel more approachable and better connected to your partner, but you will encourage them to feel more positive about you, leading to them communicating with more positive body language in turn.

Reading Other People's Body Language

As body language is a language in and of itself, getting to know how to identify and read it in others is part of learning how to communicate well. For the most part, body language is subtle and difficult to pin down. It relies greatly on intuition in order to be understood and is influenced greatly by context. culture, and the individual performing it. Each person has their own unique way of expressing themselves through their body language, although there are movements and gestures that vary less widely across the population and tend to be the same across cultures.

As reading body language is always a subjective experience, one of the best ways to read it in the people that you talk to is to take note of what signals they give off with their body and replicate them at a later time to work out what feelings you get from performing the same gestures. This allows you to obtain insight into what it is that their body language was telling you by seeing how it makes you feel when you do the same thing. For example, if you're talking to someone and you see them stroking their chin, and looking off into the distance, do the same thing when you're alone and see what kind of feeling it gives you. For many people, this particular piece of body language is a sign of them thinking hard, especially when they have a difficult choice or decision to make. You can also take note of your own body language when certain situations occur to try to work out what it is that you're thinking and feeling that makes you perform a certain gesture at a certain time. From doing this, you can gain a level of insight into another person's mind when you see them doing the same thing.

The largely involuntary and automatic nature of body language means it can often betray our thoughts and feelings, even when we'd rather keep up different appearances and keep our internal world private. For this reason, it's important to try your best not to judge people when you see them giving off signs that might offend you, such as noticing that they don't appear to be as interested in talking to you as they were just a few minutes ago. We can't help the way we feel, and people will often do their best to be polite with their words and tone even as their body screams that they're uncomfortable or would rather not be doing whatever they're doing right now. When you pick up on these signals, you'd do well to take note but avoid addressing them, as doing this will likely only lead to difficulty and awkwardness. Communicating positively isn't about judging, but about understanding people. If you're talking to a person and you can see them shifting their weight, turning their feet, and looking somewhere else, then you could reasonably deduce that they want to end the conversation because they're distracted and their thoughts lie elsewhere. You could then do your best to bring the conversation to a close quickly, or move things on to a new topic that they show more interest in.

Showing consideration by doing this provides you with a sensitive and understanding approach to communication with another person through reading their body language. Understanding people builds a rapport between the two of you and increases the strength of the connection you have with them. If you can be sensitive enough to use your powers of communication to understand others, you will strengthen the relationships you have and make them feel better about you.

Another common feature of body language that you can read with a good degree of accuracy is by watching people's eyes and seeing where they go when you ask them a question. Unless the person has a response prepared — in which case they will tend to reply without breaking eye contact — their eyes will dart away as they think of their answer before returning to your gaze to reply. If they look up and to their left, they're engaging the left hemisphere of their brain, which is associated with facts, information, logic, and memories. If, however, they look up and to the right, a person is accessing the right-hand side of their brain. This is the region of the brain associated with creativity, imagination, and thoughts about the future. If they look to one side or the other, without an upwards slant, it usually means that they're listening to what you're saying. If they look straight down, their answer is being shaped by emotion. The longer they spend looking down, the deeper the emotion and the more emotion will be attached to their answer.

Learning to read the motions of people's eyes can help us when it comes to communicating better. It will give you an idea of the kind of place their answer stems from, and what region of their brain they've had to access to get it. The eyes also lend a lot of gravity and weight to a person's response and allow you to better judge their internal cognitive processes and understand them more thoroughly.

Quick tip: When you ask a question and sense you're going to get an answer steeped in emotion because the person you're talking to looks down, it can be tempting to try and rescue them by changing the subject or interrupting them to help them with what you think their response might be. However, you should be patient and wait for them to answer. This builds rapport, trust, and connection with the person, as you've given them the time to let them express themselves fully, no matter how difficult it might be. Let people feel what they're feeling rather than trying to save them, and your relationship with them will strengthen.

Making a Good First Impression

First impressions can be crucial at certain critical moments in our lives. If you're going to a job interview or meeting a prospective client, making a good impression can make all the difference in determining whether the outcome of your meeting is positive or negative. Likewise, if you're meeting your partner's parents for the first time or even going on a first date, you're going to want to make a good first impression. The secret to having a positive impact on people the first time you meet them is all about where your mental focus lies. When you meet someone, the interaction between the two of you generates a focus in each of your minds that determines how you feel about that interaction. Broadly speaking, the most important focus of each person at that time is how each individual feels about themselves, and how each feels about the other person, i.e.:

- **How you feel about yourself**

- **How you feel about the other person**

- **How they feel about themselves**

- **How they feel about you**

The interaction between the two of you will place the focus in both of your minds on one of these key areas, and will often fluctuate between them. If when you meet a person for the first time you're focusing on how you feel about yourself, you'll tend to feel self-conscious and make a poor first impression because you're anxious, self-critical, and you end up second-guessing yourself and not focusing on the conversation. This can potentially be devastating for your first impression. If your focus is instead on how the other person feels about you, you will be trying too hard to please them, and you'll come across as fake or insecure. If you're thinking about and focusing on how you feel about the other person, the first impression that they are likely to receive of you is that you are critical or judgmental, which is obviously something that you want to avoid. If, however, your focus is on how the other person feels about themselves, the chances are that you'll make a good first impression. This is where you should try to keep the focus of the interaction in your mind, regardless of the context of the first meeting. When your own mind is focused on how the other person feels about themselves, you create a genuine and positive impression on them.

Example: You meet a potential new client at work and you want to make a good impression. You take them out for lunch. Now, you could either talk about yourself, in which case the focus of both you and them will be on you, or you can influence the conversation to be about them, which would switch the focus onto them instead. You can then ask probing questions in order to work out how they feel about themselves, others, and the events of their life, putting the focus exactly where you want it to be in order for them to feel great about you. To them, you're one of the nicest and most genuinely interested people they've ever met, and to you, they're a new client!

Chapter Two: Relationships At Work

The area in which the average person will spend a large amount of their life and the one which is crucial in determining their income, satisfaction, and well-being in the workplace. Most people spend about eight hours a day at work, five days a week, for the vast majority of the year. This means that if the relationships you have with the people you work with are poor, you're probably going to be miserable for a significant portion of your life. A negative state of mind at work will seep into and permeate the other parts of your life, which, if left unchecked, can end up making you into a bitter and resentful person. There are two main categories to keep in mind when it comes to managing and improving the relationships you have at work.

The Importance of Positivity in the Workplace

When it comes to maintaining good relationships through communication at work, positivity is the key. This is true of both the attitude that you as an individual bring to your work and the atmosphere of the workplace itself. As a member of your workplace, you are one of the people that generate that atmosphere, and you're partly responsible for how welcoming and supportive your workplace feels.

Having good relationships with the people you work with is a vital part of your individual success, as well as that of the company. Happiness and success are closely linked, although not in the way that a lot of people think they are. Many people think that the more successful a person is, the happier they will be, but in reality, the opposite is true; the happier someone is, the more successful they tend to be. The link between work life and happiness, however, is a tangible one. If you work in a stressful and negative environment, you're going to be stressed and negative for a large proportion of your life — this inevitably seeps into your home life and forms the outlook and mindstate that you wake up with every day.

A big part of any working environment are your co-workers, the people you interact with every day and work closely with. If your attitude to work is negative, the relationships you have with your coworkers and therefore the atmosphere of your workplace will be negative, and if the atmosphere of your workplace is negative, your attitude towards it will be negative, too. The effect of this vicious cycle of negativity is poor relationships with the people you work with, which leads to conflict and resentment and makes the workplace an even more hostile place to be. It's for this very reason that positivity in the workplace is so important. If you're positive, your workplace is likely to be a more positive place. You will feel happier and more fulfilled, and you will have better relationships with the people that you work with, as well as being more successful.

The benefits of positivity in the workplace are immeasurable and extend to employers as well as employees. It increases productivity; just look at companies like Google that know how to keep their employees happy, because they know that happy employees are productive employees, and enhanced productivity results in a better bottom line. A positive workplace will generate more profit for a company than a negative one. A positive work environment also leads to a reduction of employee turnover and better worker retention, meaning the best employees stick around and improve the workplace even further by setting a high standard and helping to generate a great atmosphere.

One of the most common reasons people give for wanting to leave jobs is a toxic workplace; it makes being at work a highly unpleasant and caustic experience. Research that has been conducted over the last couple of decades by the Journal of Occupational Health Psychology has strongly linked negative and toxic workplace environments with increased rates of depression and substance abuse. Enhancing your own mindset and attitude towards your place of work through your own positivity will help to spur the same thing on in other people, gradually influencing the atmosphere of the whole company and ensuring that the time you spend at work is better for yourself and for all of your co-workers.

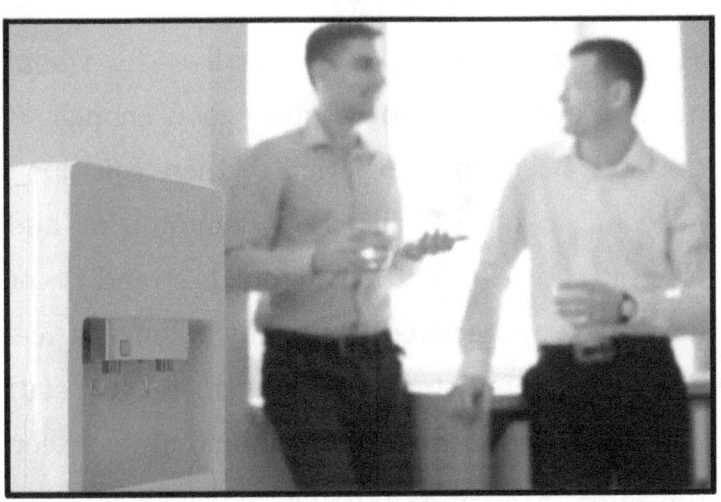

If you're an employer or you're responsible for other members of staff at your place of work, positivity can be applied in two main ways to enhance the productivity of both yourself and the people around you, and as a result the company. If your team is bringing in good numbers, it will reflect well on you and improve your position within the company, bringing you and the people you work with new opportunities. It's a win-win. Here's how to put positivity into practice:

Positive Evaluation

Lots of people can relate to having a figure of authority at some point in their lives for whom nothing ever seems to be quite good enough. If this has been your experience, then you don't need me to tell you just how demoralizing and frustrating it can be to give your best and never have it be appreciated, especially when you feel like you're doing great work. When you give staff appraisals and feedback, you should always keep things as positive as possible and let your staff know that you appreciate their efforts. Always fill them in on how their actions have been beneficial for the company, and show your gratitude for their hard work as often as possible. Tell them that they're doing well and that they should be proud of themselves for their achievements.

It can be tempting when evaluating your staff to say 'You're doing brilliantly, but it could be better.' This attitude stems from a place of understanding that there is always room for improvement and from a desire to do as well as possible. The problem with doing this, though, is that it undermines the confidence of your staff in their own ability. People can always be doing better, no matter how excellent their performance is. Using the word 'but' after praising your staff and following it with the suggestion that they could do better erodes any chance for them to actually enjoy the positive feedback they've just received. Dangling the carrot of appreciation only to snatch it back and inform them that they could be doing more will have a net negative effect on the morale of your workers. Instead, allow the positivity to linger and be fully absorbed by your staff by thanking and praising them without encouraging them to work any harder, for now. Allow them the chance to bask in the brilliant warmth of the feeling of doing well by pausing and delivery positive creativity separately.

Positive Creativity

After you've made sure you're positively evaluating your staff, you can begin to encourage positive creativity in addition to praising and thanking them. Essentially, all this consists of is separating the encouragement to do better from the statement that they're doing well. Rather than saying 'but you could do better', try to instead frame any encouragement separately from the praise offered. You can always push your staff on to the next level by incentivizing them to do even better for even more reward. You need to try and phrase it as though they have the chance to move on to something even better than what they already have in order to build energy, pride, and hope. This enables them to move forward and create something even better through harnessing the energy and creativity provided by a positive workplace.

If you're an employee rather than an employer or manager, you still have every motivation to make your workplace as positive a place to be as you can through your own positive attitude. For one thing, a happier workplace will make you a happier person. When you feel calm and at peace in your place of work, you are relaxed and fulfilled rather than being stressed or anxious about your performance. Positivity, therefore, isn't just about the workplace. It carries over into every aspect of your life; your relationships, your finances, your family, and your general wellbeing will all soar as a result of being happier and more satisfied in your work.

Quick tip: Bringing a more positive attitude to work with you will also bring you new opportunities in the form of raises and promotions. Your bosses will notice your enhanced productivity and your morale-boosting effect on the team. You will draw attention to yourself as exactly the kind of person who your company wants and needs — someone with a great attitude and work ethic. Someone who gets things done. This will bring you new chances that you didn't expect. Doors open, conversations happen, and things begin to move quickly for you as a result of your initiative. You build new relationships with people that will carry you further and further on in life, giving you the opportunity to put your communication skills to the test and make the most of the new opportunities that you bring to yourself.

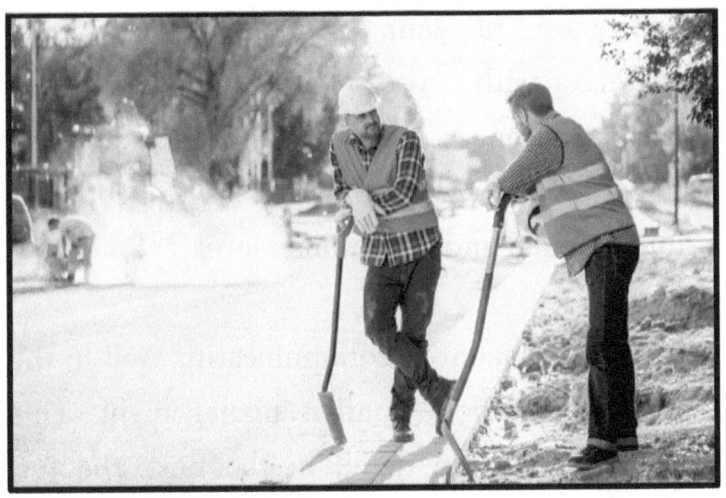

Communication in the Workplace

Good communication is absolutely vital to good professional and business practice. It's essential in building the relationships that these things are based around at their core — as any successful business person will tell you, having the right connections makes all the difference, and building the right connections involves being a good communicator. It's also an essential factor in building and sustaining relationships with clients, increasing profitability and the effectiveness of your team, and successfully engaging with your employees. Positive communication is about far more than just talking, too; it's about connecting with people on a fundamental and very human level.

A large component of communicating well in the workplace is about conflict management. This will be covered in detail in the next chapter, which will deal with managing conflict in relationships in all of the other areas of your life as well as the workplace.

Enhanced employee engagement is one of the most beneficial results of positive communication in the workplace. That is to say, employees feel more connected to and a greater degree of personal investment in their place of work when they have positive relationships with their coworkers and management. When employees are more engaged in the workplace, they align more closely with the company's goals and objectives and help the whole enterprise to become more efficient and more productive. They also gain a greater understanding of each other, which means skills and talents that may otherwise have gone unnoticed can be highlighted and cultivated within the work environment to get the most use out of them by using individuals in the roles that they most excel in. This results in a more talented and productive workforce.

Good communication in the workplace has a number of other benefits for both employees and their employers. It leads to a more open work culture, better suited to innovation and creative thought. It enhances team building and gives everyone a voice, leading to better employee satisfaction, higher morale, and a much more positive place of work. It allows for better growth and management, and better efficiency when it comes to the use of resources.

Improving Communication in the Workplace

Putting better communication into practice in the workplace requires focusing on a few key areas of consideration:

- **Well - defined goals and expectations** - Objectives and aims need to be clearly ratified by both management and employees. Staff should know exactly what it is that is expected of them and should have their own goals and expectations of themselves that they share with management. Any goals set should be achievable in order to boost morale; setting unrealistic goals only leads to disappointment when people are inevitably unable to deliver on them. All members of staff should be aware of the objectives of every project and the organization as a whole.

- **Clearly delivered messages** - All items of communication should be clear, easily understandable, and accessible to everyone that needs to see it. It's important to speak both plainly and politely to ensure that your message is clearly understood and won't cause any confusion or hurt anyone's feelings. You should also consider the medium through which your message will be expressed. While face-to-face conversations are usually the best way to pass on messages, sometimes other means are required, such as emails or written notes. Take the time to think about the best way to get your message across to the right people.

- **Inclusivity and involvement** - It's vital that everyone in the workplace feels heard and included. Everyone should be kept up to date. If people are left out of the loop and miss out on important news and information, they will feel excluded. Part of involving everyone in the workplace is taking the time to listen to everyone and have constantly open lines of communication so that everyone has a voice. Communication is a two-way street, so feedback should always be valued and respected. Fostering an open atmosphere in the workplace leads to a greater level of mutual trust and respect amongst all of the individual members of the team, resulting in greater overall performance.

Chapter Three: Managing Conflict

An important part of becoming a good communicator and learning to better manage the relationships you have is learning how to deal with conflict. Unfortunately, conflict is a fact of life. People butt heads and have disagreements all the time, over virtually anything, and if you want to be successful at communicating positively it's vital that you learn how to manage conflict properly and appropriately so that you can take charge of tricky situations and steer them in the right direction, no matter the context that they occur in.

Managing Conflict at Work

Conflict can be particularly difficult to deal with when it occurs in the workplace. Tension and open conflict reduce productivity and efficiency and create a negative and toxic working environment. The majority of conflict and nearly all preventable conflict stems from a lack of good communication. It is therefore essential that you do your best to nip any conflict in the bud early and prevent it from arising by establishing good communication with and amongst the people you work with and with and amongst any employees that you're responsible for.

In general, conflict at work tends to boil down to a deep-running pattern of misunderstanding and miscommunication among employees that sparks up into more obvious conflict because of certain stressful circumstances or events. Many employees will tolerate less than adequate communication from certain individuals so as not to make a scene or cause any drama, meaning conflict can appear to come out of nowhere when flashpoints occur that set off a chain reaction fuelled and exacerbated by pent-up negative feelings. Communication is tricky at the best of times, but it's even harder when stressful situations occur. Maintaining a positive atmosphere that seeks to alleviate and minimize stress for everyone will prevent the likelihood of such situations occurring in the first place and will reduce the severity of them when they do. If all employees understand that there's no need or place for drama at work, they will be more likely to sit down and talk things out sensibly and patiently rather than letting their emotions get the better of them and causing a toxic atmosphere.

Most conflict comes down to misunderstandings because of miscommunication. Even when people feel like they're communicating well, it is difficult to for them to know whether or not they actually are unless they have a good understanding of the communication style of the people that they're talking to. if they're speaking to someone with a different communication pattern, both parties may end up walking away with very different ideas about what is expected of them and how to go about doing it. This can lead to issues down the line, particularly if there are serious consequences to this miscommunication and people feel like their jobs are on the line, in which case they're likely to become defensive. Acknowledging that everyone has different communication patterns and styles through group meetings and training sessions can be a great way to cultivate a greater understanding of the subtle differences in the ways people process and understand information. Doing this can also be used as a way to allow people to figure out the communication patterns of the people they work with, and to emphasize the importance of double checking that both sides fully understand something before going away to work on it.

More serious causes of conflict in workplace environments include people feeling disregarded, like their emotional needs aren't being met, and that they're being taken advantage of and manipulated. When conflict erupts around these issues, it can be more difficult and complicated to resolve, particularly if there's a significant air of tension in the aftermath. Laying good foundations of communication and having little tolerance for unfair or malignant behavior in the workplace will help to prevent this kind of conflict from occurring in the first place.

When conflict does break out, the first priority for everyone present should be to de-escalate tension and end the immediate conflict as soon as possible. Once this has been achieved, a period of acknowledgment, communication, and repair to damaged relationships is vital to resolving both the root cause and any symptoms of conflict and allowing things to return to normal. This can be achieved by management and HR stepping in to mediate and allow all parties involved speaking about and coming to a resolution on the topics that caused conflict in the first place. A key part of this process is acknowledging and embracing the fact that conflict occurred in the first place, rather than taking steps to bury or hide it.

Quick tip: Sometimes, you will find yourself at the center of conflict quite by accident. Managing conflict for yourself at work is mostly about the attitude you take towards it. You should always attempt to maintain composure and professionalism by putting the job first and making sure you follow the appropriate steps to report any negative, toxic, or unprofessional behavior as soon as possible through the appropriate channels. Don't allow yourself to be dragged down if someone is being intentionally difficult or antagonistic by responding in kind. The ability to keep a cool head and think clearly in stressful situations will set you apart and help you to advance in your own role as well as managing any conflict that you find yourself a part of in a positive manner.

Dealing With Negative People

Everybody has negative people in their lives, and everybody is negative from time to time. It's part of being human. However, some people are more negative than others, to the point where they have a consistently toxic effect on the lives of the people around them for one reason or another. The important thing to understand here is that negativity almost always stems from deep emotional pain. People that are hurting inside act out and hurt the people around them in ways that aren't necessarily typical for them. The best way to deal with negative people in your life is, therefore, to approach them with a kind, compassionate, and empathetic mindset. You should always try to treat people the way you'd like to be treated, regardless of how they treat you.

For a lot of negative people, treating others poorly is a self-defense mechanism meant to help preserve themselves in the face of what they see as threats to themselves, for whatever reason. It doesn't excuse their behavior, but it does help to explain it. When people feel cornered, they act out. The most negative people are people who are in a great deal of pain that they don't know how to deal with. Most people are just doing the best they can with the information they have at hand at any one time.

Dealing with negative people in the right way is first and foremost about changing your own attitude, mindstate and opinions on them. Put yourself in a position to observe, rather than judging them, and prevent yourself from engaging in the negativity. Try to be interested in understanding people rather than focusing on how much you dislike or disapprove of their negative traits. At the end of the day, no one has the power to unpick the riddles of a person's life. Circumstances manifest themselves to us and situations unfold in such a way that we're often unable to see a better way of doing things because we're too hung up on the things causing us pain.

Instead of writing people off or judging them, we can see them as the fascinating and troubled people that they are. If you can learn to see things in this way, you'll find that you're in a very powerful position; it doesn't change you, cost you, or alter your course through life to allow people to do their thing. It simply helps you to understand them.

Taking this perspective is an incredibly helpful and empowering technique when it comes to dealing with the negative people in your life. It's a way to let yourself to be in the presence of negativity without allowing it to affect your own mood and mindstate. Try to take the position with yourself that negativity doesn't have any control over you unless you allow it to. It isn't the boss of you, and you don't become negative unless you give your negativity the room it needs to breathe. In order for your mindstate and mood to become negative, you first have to hand over your emotional life and positivity. You always have the choice of allowing any negative feelings to dissipate rather than indulging them. You get to choose and maintain your own position in life. You decide how positive or negative your outlook is and make a certain attitude your own. It's a good idea to choose one that serves you well and makes you happy. You don't have to give in to the attempts from negative people to make you buy into their negative mindset.

> **Quick tip:** choosing to treat the negative people around you with love and kindness doesn't mean that you have to allow yourself to be walked over. Distance is necessary for any relationship, and if someone is having a negative effect on you, you owe it to yourself and your own happiness to be able and prepared to put a bit of distance between them and you. Be brave and be kind, and don't let people take you away from your resolution to be kind,

> loving, and to act with integrity, because those things come from inside, not from what other people observe. You don't need anyone else's permission or validation to be happy within yourself.

How to Deal With Toxic Relationships

Toxic people can take many different shapes and forms in your life. You might run into a toxic person at a grocery store who snaps at you because they're having a bad day, or you might have a toxic friend, partner, sibling, or parent that you can't simply walk away from because they're a big part of your life. Toxic behavior varies widely, from simple pettiness and small minded attitudes to persistent bullying and manipulation. Handling toxic people and relationships is complicated as a result of this, so we're going to break it down into subcategories in order to more comprehensively address the toxic situations you're likely to face in your own life.

Handling Toxic Interactions

Toxic interactions are those conversations and experiences we have with people that leave us feeling significantly worse than we felt beforehand. In this way, they can be compared to having a brush with a venomous plant or animal — think about how it feels to graze your leg against stinging nettles, where there's an initial sharp jolt of pain that's followed by irritation and burning over time. The same applies to have a brush with a toxic person. Dealing with toxic interactions can be handled in a very similar way to how you'd respond to being stung.

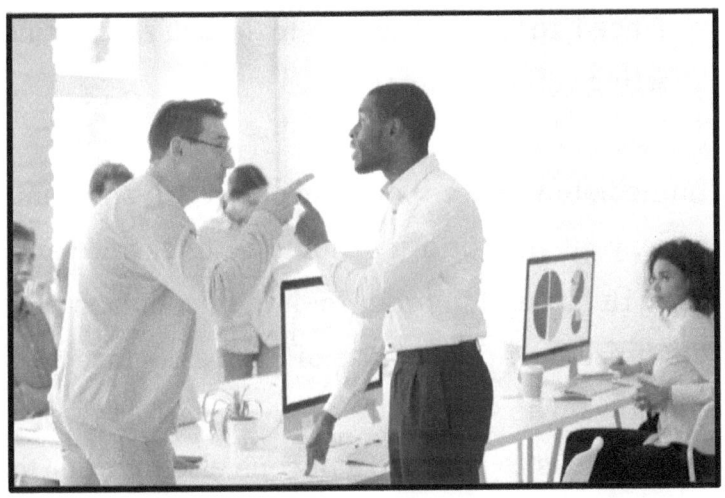

The first stage in handling toxic interactions is actually a precautionary and pre-emptive one. You can build resilience to toxic experiences by practicing self-care such as getting enough sleep, exercising regularly, and eating a healthy and nutritious diet. Looking after yourself by doing these things will serve to bolster and fortify you mentally, meaning that you'll be less affected by having a brush with someone toxic. Their behavior will be more likely to break on you like water on a rock without crippling you or making you crumble internally because you're doing what you need to do to prevent toxic behavior from affecting you more intensely.

Immediately after being exposed to someone toxic, your first priority should be to cleanse and rinse the wound in order to dilute the poison and minimize the initial effects of having contact with someone who's toxic. A good way to approach doing this is to speak to someone else in order to get the experience off of your chest and stop it from slowly eating at you internally in isolation. Confirming with another person that the behavior you were on the receiving end of was, in fact, toxic can help you to feel less alone and less like a victim of the experience you had. You can then start to try and put things in perspective. When we've just had a horrible interaction with someone, we tend to feel overwhelmed by what's happened. It's all that we can think about, so we dwell on it and build it up in our minds until it morphs into something that it isn't in reality. It can, therefore, be very helpful to step back and see the bigger picture, to see that in the grand scheme of things, a toxic interaction doesn't really mean much at all. It's awful at the time when we can't see the forest because of the trees, but some distance and perspective helps us to see these things as they really are.

The second stage is to remove the poison in order to go back to a more healthy and positive mindset. This can take the form of self-help measures like positivity training, or more professional avenues such as therapy or counseling. The goal is to condition your mind in order to frame past negative experiences in a different way so that you're able to package them away having learned all the lessons from them that you can, and then move on with it being just another part of your past like anything else. Changing the attitude you have to the negative and toxic things that have happened to you allows you to become comfortable with having had them and able to move on without them weighing you down, something which can be an incredibly liberating experience.

Another factor in healing after you've had an interaction with someone who is toxic is evaluating the type of people you want to surround yourself with. This is especially important when the person you had a negative or toxic experience with is someone who you're close with or see a lot of. If this is the case, you might want to consider putting some distance between yourself and them or even letting them go from your life altogether if that isn't enough. Our personalities tend to be an average of the five people that we hang out with the most, which means that if we spend a lot of time with negative or toxic people we will experience an amount of their negative personality and toxic behavior rubbing off on us and becoming a part of who we are. Obviously, this isn't something that any of us want to happen, so we have to be able to defend ourselves, our happiness, wellbeing, and emotional lives from people whose presence would affect us negatively, whether intentionally or not. We have to strive to forge positive, inspiring, and uplifting relationships in our lives that enhance and enrich us in order to attain new levels of peace and wellbeing that counteract negative people and experiences.

People Who Take Advantage of You

Chances are, you've experienced what it's like to have people try to manipulate or take advantage of you. If you don't, you will eventually. It's a part of life as a social animal. A lot of people see this in a very negative and pessimistic manner. They see it as a symptom of people's selfishness and greed that we can twist people into doing what we want so that we can benefit from it. Accepting that there are people out there who will try and succeed in taking advantage of you can be a liberating feeling, though, as it means that you're in a much better position to see the warning signs when a person has their eyes on you so that you can try to prevent it from happening by putting yourself in a position to avoid it or reduce the effect it has on you.

Once someone has their claws into you and is actively taking advantage of or manipulating you, it can be very difficult to deal with. Stopping a person from taking advantage of you in the first place can be hard enough, but when they've already twisted the knife enough to begin to see rewards, they will only double down and fight back against your attempts to free yourself from their grasp. The weapons a manipulator can wield are varied, but they usually involve attempts to make you feel guilty or like you're letting them down by refusing to go out of your way to help them, as well as gaslighting you by swearing that your memory is wrong and that their version of events is correct, even if you know for a fact that it's not. An example of this is if your partner takes advantage of you by letting you cook their meals, gets annoyed and upset when you even suggest that perhaps they take a turn cooking for you both, and says that you're the reason that they're upset and that if you just made them dinner you'd stop making their life difficult, and then gaslights you by assuring you that you agreed to make them dinner tonight, although you know you didn't. Yeah. Fun stuff.

The important thing to remember here is that you don't owe anyone anything. Kind and compassionate people make the best targets for people looking to gain from other people's losses, as they can often be pushed further and faster than less empathetic individuals who will shut down attempts to take advantage of them quickly and then stand their ground. If you're being mistreated — no matter who it is that's doing it — you don't have to put up with it. It's something that you've allowed to happen, even if you haven't noticed before now that it's abusive. The world can be a harsh and unforgiving place, and some of the things that you have to do in order to take care of yourself will be things that you don't want to do, things that you're afraid to do; at the end of the day, you have to do them in order to be a happy and well-adjusted person. You have to be kind and brave, and make sure you do what has to be done to put yourself first and stop yourself being manipulated by cunning, calculating predators that would use you for their own self-interest.

For a lot of people, confronting the person or people that they're being mistreated or taken advantage of by seems worse than just putting up with them and doing what they want. Being afraid of confrontation isn't a bad thing, but it will hold you back from being truly fulfilled by your life if you let it. Being brave isn't about not being scared. It's about feeling scared and terrified and afraid to do something and then doing it anyway. Life is a game of risk and chance. You might not be listened to, you might be rejected or overridden, but it doesn't matter. You have to be prepared to stand up for yourself, to have the courage and tell yourself that you're not willing to put up with being anyone's puppet any longer.

When a relationship is unhealthy or toxic, you have to have boundaries and limits that outline what is and isn't okay for you, and what you're unwilling to put up with from other people. Ask yourself what positions you're willing to put yourself in. Setting out these boundaries and enforcing them doesn't feel like a particularly nice thing to do, but it is necessary. It certainly isn't pleasant, but neither are many of the things that we have to do in life in order to survive, blossom and thrive. The simple truth is that life is one big learning experience. It's an opportunity for growth, and growth isn't something that happens when you never leave the safety of your comfort zone. If you're comfortable, you're not growing. If you want to progress as a person, you have to allow yourself to get out of your depth from time to time in order to push your boundaries. You are in control of the relationships you have with people. You get to determine what type of relationship you have with them and how close or distant you are. You get to decide how much you're willing to give to any one person, and therefore the extent to which people are able to take advantage of you in the first place.

You have to learn to assert yourself in order to protect yourself from toxic exposure and manipulation. This doesn't mean that you have to be aggressive; you can be assertive while remaining kind and calm. Being assertive is about sending a clear message to the people around you that you're not willing to put up with their attempts at controlling you or bringing you down and indicating that you're prepared to defend yourself from them if necessary. It's okay to opt out of a conversation when it isn't working for you. It's okay to walk away from dialogue, an event, a situation, or anything that makes you uncomfortable or just isn't what is best for you at any given time. You don't owe anyone an explanation for doing what you have to do to take care of yourself. Put yourself first, because that's what you have to do in order to survive and be happy in this world.

Setting limits and boundaries can involve any number of things, and is highly dependent on the nature of the relationship that you have with someone. Most importantly, you get to decide what these limits are. They're non-negotiable. If you're not comfortable with something, then set a boundary. If your friend relies on you to bail them out of trouble financially, then tell them that you won't lend them any more money — and then stick to your word. Setting boundaries and limits are useless if you're not prepared to enforce them. If you've drawn a line in the sand and someone crosses it, you need to be ready to take action and show them that their behavior has consequences. If all you do is make empty threats that you're not willing to carry out, you will be taken advantage of as soon as the people that use you get wise to your reluctance to enforce strict boundaries. They'll test you to see how you react, then pile on whatever they can get if they smell blood.

Once you're actually setting boundaries, you'll find that you come to a 'make or break' situation in your relationship with a manipulative person. This is where you get to decide whether to renew the relationship and start again with a fresh dynamic and different expectations and rules, or leave it behind entirely and move on without that person in your life. The choice you make here will be highly dependent on the type of relationship you have with a person; it's much easier to leave a former friend behind than it is to cut ties with your parents. If you believe that the relationship is salvageable or too important to let go, then you have to be committed to making it change so that it's no longer unhealthy or toxic. You have to reinvent the relationship in order to make it work on terms that are acceptable for you. The old relationship has to be left behind in its entirety. You can't go back to the way things were, because if that wasn't working for you before it never will. If you can't have a healthy relationship with someone, it might be time to consider releasing them from your life so that you can move on and surround yourself with more positive and supportive people. Release them and have them become part of your past, rather than a part of your present or your future. It's okay to let people go. Being a part of your life is a privilege you grant to people, not their right. If it's not feasible, practical, or possible for a person to remain in your life, you have every right to let them leave.

Perhaps the most important part of managing a difficult or manipulative relationship with someone is learning how to really practice forgiveness. Whether you decide to keep such a person as a part of your life on new terms or you have to let them go, you have to be able to forgive them. That doesn't mean that you're excusing their abusive behavior or advantage-taking; you're not letting them off the hook or pardoning them for their wrongs. You're not making yourself out to be weak or opening the door for yourself to be manipulated again in the future, either. What you're doing is you're leaving the emotional baggage you've accumulated as a result of this person in the past where it belongs, rather than carrying it with you into the future. Forgiveness is about leaving the burden of their memory behind so that you can go forward in peace.

Dealing with relationships of a toxic or abusive nature is always difficult, but it can be particularly hard to handle when it's someone that you're in a romantic relationship with. Being so close with someone can sometimes blind us to their negative side and allows them to get away with things that we wouldn't otherwise tolerate from anyone else, particularly if the abuse is subtle and emotional in nature rather than physical. This makes it all the more important that you take note of any red flags and seek advice about the relationship from friends or family whenever you feel the need to. Toxic and abusive romantic relationships often involve the abuser cutting their victim off from their support network, so keep an eye out for controlling and dominant behavior like attempts to restrict who you can and can't talk to.

Handling Toxic Friends, Partners, and Family Members

Toxic people can take any role in your life. They can be your friend, your parents, and your siblings. Sometimes, we might not even realize that someone is toxic until we've gotten to know them well over a number of years, at which point they're entrenched in our lives and are difficult to remove. A hard fact of life is that the people closest to you are the people most capable of hurting you. These are the people who have the most access to you and the most power over you. The fact that you're close with them emotionally and in terms of physical proximity means that you can't just simply cut them out of your life easier at the first sign of trouble, and toxic individuals will use this to their advantage to stay close to you and fill your life with their corrosive venom.

A common feature of toxic behavior is putting others down frequently for no apparent reason, which is a characteristic that can be incredibly draining and hurtful for those on the receiving end of it. Although it might seem like these put-downs have no apparent cause or motivation, they're often the result of people feeling negative about their own lives and making themselves feel better by insulting others. Additionally, some people get a sick sense of satisfaction out of making others feel bad. When they see their words having a serious effect on other people, they feel powerful and strong. They might like to control or dominate the feelings of others in order to make themselves feel good. This kind of behavior is indicative of emotional abuse, and can sometimes be pathological in nature, meaning it stems from a mental illness or disorder.

The main thing to keep in mind when addressing toxic behavior from people close to you is that most of the time, the reason for you being put down or bullied is that the perpetrator is looking for a reaction from you that makes them feel good. Your reaction, although not your fault, of course, is what perpetuates the behavior and closes the loop, forming a vicious circle of toxicity. In order to break the cycle, you have to change the way you react to the put-downs and insults that are aimed at you. You can do this by taking an inventory of your own behavior and noticing how you react to constant and consistent criticism or putdowns. When you're hurt and annoyed, you're likely to get defensive. This reaction is exactly what a toxic person thrives on. When you react like this, you're giving them exactly what they want. If you can train yourself to disconnect your reaction from the stimuli, you can instead respond with something neutral or even completely ignore the insult. Without the response they're looking for, the perpetrator has little incentive to keep putting you down and will eventually get bored and stop.

> **Quick tip:** A good way to deal with this kind of toxic behavior and assess whether or not it stems from a place of malignancy or simply a lack of self-awareness is to use a strategy called 'identify, verify, accept'. The first step here is to identify exactly how you feel about being exposed to the negative and toxic behavior that you're experiencing. You can then verify that this is how the person wanted you to feel by explaining to them how their behavior makes you feel and asking them if that was their intention. The

response to this that you will receive can range from sudden realization and heartfelt apologies to denial, such as saying that you're just overly sensitive and it's your fault that you're upset. No matter the response you receive, the final stage is to accept it. You've let them know by confronting them that the way they're treating you has an impact on you andyou're not willing to put up with it. The way you proceed is up to you but should involve an amount of reflection and assessment of the kind of relationship you want to have with that person. As I've indicated previously if they're not a positive influence on your life, you should think long and hard about the kind of distance you want to maintain from them and whether or not you want to have such a toxic and corrosive influence as part of your life.

Chapter Four: Becoming A Better Listener

When it comes to communication, there is no skill more important than the ability to listen. It's the key to all good communication. It comes more easily to some people than to others, though. A lack of good listening and communication hinders relationships significantly. They can't be positive or of any real substance or depth without it.

How to Become a Better Listener

Women tend to be natural listeners than men, and can usually practice the skill far better than their male counterparts. Like any skill, however, you can learn to become better at listening by working hard on it. With a little bit of direction and effort, you can learn how to become a better listener in order to open up new relationships with people in key areas of your life as well as improving your current ones and reforging old bonds.

Listen More Effectively

Effective listening consists of the ability to focus on what's being said. All communication is essentially a process of a sender, or speaker, encoding information to be decoded by a receiver, or listener. If a listener understands not only what a speaker is saying, but fully grasps the wider point they're trying to make, communication between the two of them has been successful. Learning to listen more effectively means actively working to improve in a few key areas in order to make sure that you decode information correctly and grasp the point the speaker is trying to make as well as you possibly can. Your job as a listener is to understand, not to agree. You simply have to try and get where they're coming from and hear them fully, one human to another, regardless of whether or not you personally agree with the content of the communication.

Mental focus is important here. You need to concentrate all of your attention on keeping up with what is being said, rather than allowing yourself to think about other things or letting your attention wander or be distracted. This can be very difficult to do at times, particularly when you're in a busy or loud environment where there's a lot of different stimuli that your mind will want to pay attention to rather than what's being said by the person that you're trying to listen to. If the conversation is important, it's always a good idea to make sure that the two of you are somewhere quiet in order for you to have the chance to properly listen to what is being said.

It's a common misconception that good listening requires total silence on the part of the listener. In fact, total silence makes it harder for both parties to communicate, as the speaker will need verbal and visual cues such as positive affirmations of understanding, eye contact, and head nods in order to confirm that what they've said has been understood. Without these things, speakers tend to start to second guess themselves and wonder if their audience is paying attention or just off somewhere else mentally. If you're making a real effort to understand, you can acknowledge what is being said by giving the speaker these indications that you understand; this process is known as reflective listening and is one of the single greatest things you can do in order to enhance your listening skills. When you practice reflective listening, you'll see the speaker light up and be reassured by your attentiveness, helping give them the courage to express themselves fully and properly as they know it will be properly heard and received. When you're properly understanding what a speaker is trying to say, your reflective listening will be met with enthusiasm and confirmation from the speaker that you're grasping their meaning. Likewise, if you're misunderstanding them, they will hesitate, reiterate their points in different words, and help you to understand them better wherever there are points of contention.

While you shouldn't stay silent, effective listening *is* about listening more than you speak. You have two ears and one mouth, and you should try to use them in roughly this ratio as much as you possibly can. If you have a point you want to make or you feel like you have the answer a person is looking for, wait for your turn to speak. Don't rush in and interrupt them; speaking isn't your role when you're listening. Your role is to understand, and there will come a time where you can make any points you might have to them all at once. You might even find that listening to them completely negates the need to make some of your points or even changes what you want to say entirely.

Listening is an extremely powerful tool. If you're ever in a meeting with a great communicator, you'll notice that they listen attentively and wait until everyone else has spoken before they take their turn to speak. This is because they understand the value of listening, of opening their ears and their mind. It allows them to make a statement only once they've heard what everyone else has to say, meaning they're working with more information than anyone else had and can construct a far more comprehensive and powerful response. Having the patience to wait until last and then speaking impressively also lend these people a great deal of importance and respect in the eyes of those around them, who will see them as the most intelligent person in the room when really they're just a very effective listener.

When we don't listen properly, we end up receiving a flawed understanding of what the speaker is trying to get across to us. This can lead to us making assumptions that don't hold water and to unnecessary and avoidable disagreements, frustration, and conflicts between listener and speaker. If we instead give people space and time to be fully understood through listening patiently and with our full attention, we can have far more efficient and effective communication. Listening properly requires your full attention — you can't listen to someone and do anything else at the same time. Giving people the time and space to be fully understood will also directly benefit you when it's your turn to speak as it will very likely be reciprocated by the person that you just listened to.

Listen More Empathetically

Becoming a better listener is also about learning to listen more empathetically. This involves making a real, tangible connection with the speaker through using empathy to vividly imagine the way they feel about whatever it is they're talking about. Learning to listen more empathetically is harder than learning how to listen more effectively. While there are some directly applicable tools and methods to doing this, it also involves having a genuine, fundamental desire to connect with and understand the person speaking. This is a skill that can't be taught. It has to come from within, from a place far deeper than that needed to access more superficial levels of caring like just trying to pay attention. It comes from having a real desire to see the beauty in every person, in having the understanding that really connecting with and understanding others is a beautiful and infinitely rewarding thing in and of itself.

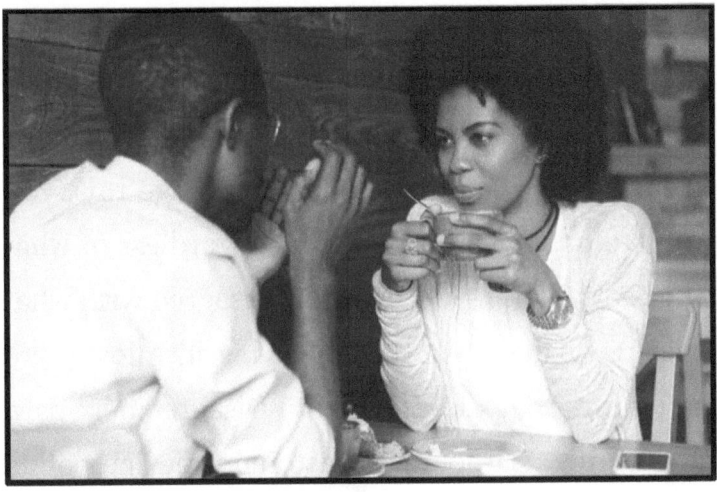

Listening empathetically is about genuinely desiring to get to know someone a bit better with every conversation, every day you spend with them. It's about valuing everything they say because it's them saying it, regardless of the content of what they say. It's about embracing your role as a listener completely and coming to love your role as the canvas onto which the speaker can paint a picture, a representation of how they feel deep inside. It's about enabling others to completely express themselves by playing the role of the listener as well as you can, with total attention and focus. It helps to be realistic and understand that no one is perfect and everyone will make mistakes or be too quick to judge someone or something or be arrogant or dismissive; when you can acknowledge this, you can stomach hearing them out regardless of what they say, even if you privately disagree with what they're saying while they're saying it. Allow there to be internal disagreement. Disagreement is a good thing. Without contrast and differing points of view, no one would think for themselves and nobody would ever learn anything. Disagreement leads to enhanced understanding when there's room for communication to take place. You will have your place to give your view on things if you're patient. When you get your opportunity after hearing them out, you can give them your advice and feedback on what they've said if you think it will help them. It helps to mentally take note of the points they're making and then address them one by one in a comprehensive way.

Quick tip: Part of listening empathetically is understanding that miscommunication will happen on both your and the speaker's parts; it's just a natural part of the act of communication between two imperfect and fallible people. Patience and effort are therefore vitally important parts of the communication process in order to compensate for this. Take the time to listen to the people that you want to maintain a good relationship with. Make the mental space necessary to put yourself into their shoes and imagine what it is they're feeling and why. Ask them questions where you feel like you should, make them feel comfortable, and look them in the eyes. If you do all of these things, you will be well on your way to becoming a better listener.

Important Tools For Better Communication

Improving your communication is a matter of putting in a good amount of effort as well as having a grasp of the skills, techniques, and tools that facilitate positive and healthy communication. In order to know how to communicate well, you first have to have a thorough understanding of communication itself. One of the key things that you need to know in order to really understand how communication works are that all communication is relative. We communicate through interpretation; we hear something and understand it through how we relate it to other things that we already understand. For example, if you were trying to explain something new to someone, you'd compare and relate it to things you know they already understand in order to help them see what you mean. If you were trying to explain how a sport works, you might compare it to another, similar sport that the person is already familiar with in order to help them shape the concept that you're trying to communicate in their mind. As a result of this interpretation, no message is ever received and decoded without an element of bias. We fill in the gaps in our knowledge by working off of things that we're already familiar with. This means that the message we think we receive is never the objective reality, but rather our own individual take on it. The relative nature of communication means that we always pass things through the filter of our own interpretation in order to understand them. In this way, communication is an active and participatory process. The speaker generates meaning in the mind of the listener, but the listener can only have meaning generated based on what they already understand.

Another key factor that you should understand about communication is that speech is a part of the thought. Sometimes, we need to speak in order to tell ourselves what we think. This means that when we ask people questions that they've never thought about before, they might speak before they've thought about what to say, simply because the thought is only now just occurring to them for the first time. Take this into account when you're talking to people, and do your best to be as non-judgmental and impartial as you possibly can, both internally and externally.

In 1981, Friedemann Schulz von Thun outlined the four-sides model of communication. It proposed that every message has one or more of four facets:

1. **Fact: What I inform about (data, facts, statements, statistics)**

2. **Self-revealing: What I reveal about myself (information about the sender)**

3. **Relationship: What I think about you (information about how we get along)**

4. **Appeal: What I want to make you do (an attempt to influence the receiver)**

There is always a differing amount of emphasis on each facet from message to message, and this emphasis can be intended and perceived differently by the sender and receiver. Some messages might not have all of these facets, but all messages will have at least one of them. Additionally, facets are often implied or inferred rather than being directly stated.

For example, a child might tell their parents that their cup of juice is empty. Now, this is a fact, but it could also contain elements of the other facets. The context of a child telling their parent that their cup is empty could lead the parent to infer that their child wants their parent to fill their cup up with more juice, which would make it an appeal, although implied rather than explicitly stated. This particular message may also contain elements of the second and third facets, as it shows that the child is unable to unwilling to fill the cup up themselves, which reveals how they feel about themselves, and also indicates that they see their parents as filling this role for them.

In order to make communication more effective as either a sender or receiver of information, you can think about how a message relates to each of these facets in order to consider what the true purpose of it might be, and how we might misinterpret what another person is saying because the message doesn't always correlate closely with their intention. Another factor of this model to consider is that individual people tend to have one of four different 'types' of ears that they have trained more than the others. These different types of ears are factual, relationship, self-revelation, and appeal. Most people tend to favor one over the others, meaning that they process the messages they receive according to one of these four types of interpretation. The underlying emphasis from the sender on each of the four different facets of their message, in addition to the particular ear of the receiver, means that a great deal of meaning can effectively be lost in translation. The way in which we interpret things can, therefore, cause conflict and issues where none would have occurred if we could simply clearly see the true intention and meaning of other people. In order to communicate healthily and effectively, we need to be aware of these four facets of messages from the sender, as well as the four ears of the receiver in order to take into account how our individual differences as people can influence how we interpret a particular message. If you ever feel questioned, criticized, or insulted, consider how these factors might be influencing yourself and the person you're talking to. You might both simply be interpreting the same message in two different ways, without considering how the other person will interpret it.

Some tips for communicating better include:

- **Speak face to face** - If possible, you should always try to say what needs to be said in person, rather than writing it down in a letter, text, or email or talking over the phone. Communication is a highly personal and complex experience. There's a lot of information that can't be transferred through words alone but relies on tone and body language. If you've ever tried to be sarcastic and found that it translates poorly over text, you'll know what I mean here.

- **Find (and make) the right time** - If something is worth saying, then it's worth taking the time to say properly. Good communication isn't rushed or hurried. It takes space and time to properly express and receive a message with a minimum of misunderstanding. If you fail to allocate the appropriate time to properly communicate with the people you need to communicate well and maintain some kind of relationship with, both the messages themselves and the relationship will suffer.

- **Use technology efficiently and effectively** - Technology can be extremely useful but should be used to augment and enhance face to face communication rather than replace it completely. You can use texts and emails up to a certain point in order to arrange things and transfer data that are more easily transferred electronically than verbally but don't fall into the trap of thinking that these forms of communication are a good replacement for speaking face to face.

- **Ask for clarity if you need it** - A great deal of misunderstanding stems from people walking away from an interaction without a clear grasp of what the other person was trying to say. They might feel awkward about asking the other person to explain themselves again after they've already made the effort to do so, or may worry that the other person will be annoyed or think that they weren't paying attention. Regardless of the reason why the communication wasn't effective, the very worst thing you can do is to walk away with the wrong idea or an incomplete understanding of the message. It is always better to ask for clarity if you're uncertain; you shouldn't be ashamed at not picking up on what was being said. Communication can be incredibly difficult, and everyone experiences unsuccessful conversations from time to time. If the other person does get irritated or annoyed by your lack of understanding, remind yourself that the way they feel is up to them and that no one is perfect. Everyone makes mistakes or loses focus or fails to grasp what is being said from time to time.

- **Respect and try to understand cultural differences** - The way that we speak and the way in which we listen and understand things is shaped by the culture that we're raised in. Differences between cultures can often lead to differing interpretations of the same message, which of course can easily result in misunderstanding. Whenever you're speaking to someone with a different cultural outlook to yourself, make sure that you take the differences in culture between the two of you into account. Try to understand what they are and accommodate for them as well as you can by repeating your explanation of things in different ways and checking that they understand, as well as asking for clarification from them when you're listening.

- **Avoid communication if you're hungry, angry, stressed, or tired** - Communication is best performed when both parties feel mentally and emotionally calm and balanced. This state of mind provides a natural threshold of patience, capacity for understanding, and good-will that make communication a more pleasant, easy, and well-flowing experience. If you're hungry, tired, stressed, or angry, however, this threshold is stretched thin. It's extremely difficult to be patient and understanding when you're in a bad mood and suffering from one or more of these agitated states. Communication at such times is rarely effective and often leads to problems, so try to avoid having important conversations when you're in this state as far as you possibly can. Instead, take the time to cool off and recuperate and approach things once more when you feel like you're more up to it.

- **Tell the truth -** If you don't do your best to stick to the truth when you're talking, it can and will eventually come back to bite you. When you lie or otherwise conceal the truth from others, you only make it more difficult for yourself in the long run. People will find holes in your stories and pull them apart, leaving you in a very awkward and difficult position. Lying often involves having to lie again and again to maintain the lie, which can very quickly spiral out of control and result in you having to sustain very elaborate stories and keep track of what lies you've told in order to avoid slipping up. Not only is this an incredibly stressful way and unnecessary way to live, but it hinders effective communication, will put a strain on the relationships that you have with people and will push the people you care about away from you over time. A person is only as good as their word, and when you lose someone's confidence you lose their respect.

- **Don't bottle up how you feel** - If you sit on how you feel and conceal it from people, it won't go away. The pressure will build up and poison your mind, manifesting itself as side effects such as irritability and a lack of patience. There's only so long you can keep a lid on the way you feel, too. It will all come spilling out eventually when something happens that means you just can't contain it any longer — and this will rarely be in a situation of your choosing. It's far better to vent your feelings to the people close to you before they have a chance to build up and bring you down internally.

- **Strive to avoid complaining** - Everyone needs to vent their feelings from time to time, but there's a time, place, and context for this. If you're constantly complaining (especially to the wrong person or in the wrong context) you will come across as negative, draining and a burden. Our problems often feel overwhelming, and talking about them helps to make us feel better, but doing this excessively and in an environment not well suited to it can cause other people to not want to be around us. Everyone has problems, and everyone should be able to talk about them to get them off of their chest. If you're always complaining about yours and putting your own issues above other people's however, the next effect you have on interactions with people will be negative and others will begin to pull away from you.

- **Try and maintain a positive attitude** - Above all else, a positive attitude will take you a very long way in communication and in life. Communicating with people can be a very difficult and tiring endeavor, so approaching it with the right frame of mind is essential in order to have the patience and perseverance to see it through to the end. You have to accept that it will be difficult at times and that sometimes you won't want to do it. At the end of the day, however, it's a part of being human, and without it, you wouldn't be able to appreciate life in the same way. Embrace it completely, accept the positives and negatives, and allow yourself to take on the challenge every time.

Additional Communication Tools

We've collected a few useful tools that can help you when you're bumping heads with someone and hitting roadblocks in your communication:

- **Hold an object to speak** - This is a standard tool in a group talking therapy and for good reason; it's extremely effective. It's a relatively simple premise — in order to speak, you have to be holding onto a certain object which is passed back and forth between each participant of the conversation. This helps give people the time and space to speak their minds and gather their thoughts without being interrupted.

- **Writing certain things down in order to order thoughts or express them better** - If you or someone else is struggling to find the right words to express themselves properly, try writing down your thoughts in order to better compose yourself and think more clearly. This can be especially helpful when you're having difficult conversations where there are a lot of complex, strong emotions that have to be worked through.

- **Take time out when arguing to cool off** - If you're involved in an argument, it's always a good idea to take the time to cool off rather than plowing ahead with a conversation when voices are raised and tempers fraying. Letting yourself calm down will allow you to approach the conversation in a more even and balanced state of mind.

Communicating Through Conflict and Difficult Emotions

Communication can be difficult at the best of times, but when there is conflict and difficult emotions involved, it can be virtually impossible. You only have to cast your eye back across human history or have a look at the horrible wars and struggles across the globe today to witness the sheer destruction and terror that can occur when communication breaks down and people become resolved to use violence and force to protect their own ideas, will, and dominance on others. In order to learn about how to communicate through conflict and strong emotions, we first need to look at the background of these two things and how they combine to form such powerful complexes.

The most conflict ultimately stems from difficult emotions that are built into our very nature. Although we often like to think of ourselves as more highly evolved than and superior to the other forms of life that we share our world with because of our ability to think, talk, and use the tools to construct things, the truth is that at heart we're every bit as primitive, basic, controlled by our instincts, and driven by our feelings as every other animal on this earth. The illusions our societies and cultures create act as a mental shield, causing us to think that we're beyond being driven by such primal desires. The truth, however, is that we are genetically coded to follow our emotions and primitive urges, and there's absolutely nothing we can do about it other than an attempt to manage it and keep it in check. Although the vast majority of people think the opposite, we are not the logical, rational, reasoning creatures that we like to pretend we are. We can be all of these things to a point, but it is artificial. At heart, we are ruled by our feelings rather than thoughts. Overriding these feelings and stopping them from corrupting and clouding our view of things is next to impossible — even the most dedicated Buddhist monk will tell you that.

We are prone by our very nature to logical fallacies and multiple types of biased thinking. There's a good reason for this nature; it has kept us alive throughout millions of years of evolution. Self-interest is wired into our DNA. We each have a primal part of the brain, close to the brain stem itself, that is responsible for some of our most basic and powerful emotions such as fear and anger. These are the emotions that have helped to keep our ancestors alive since the early days of complex life forms when they were very different from the modern human form we take today. This primal part of our brain isn't able to access higher cognitive functions like thinking and reasoning; these take place in the frontal lobe.

The primal, reptilian part of our brain deals in emotions and feelings, and it's far stronger than our higher functions, meaning our feelings and emotions can easily overwhelm and overrule our ability to reason and use logic. This cognitive bias has evolved to maintain our own interests, regardless of how they affect others. As social animals, being part of a group is essential to our survival. Alone, we starve and die. Together with others, however, we can specialize and distribute labor, to the benefit of everyone. Our evolution has shaped us to reflect this priority. We are naturally prone to tribalism and an 'in versus out' group mentality, something that's also known as 'them and us' — if someone isn't part of your group and on your side, they're an enemy.

Other examples of the cognitive bias and logical fallacies that we're prone to are numerous. We're more likely to believe whatever the people around us believe, both in terms of our family and friends or peers and our wider society, cultures, and sub-cultures as a whole. This comes from our tribal instincts; if everyone is doing it, it means it's safe. If it's safe, it's not a threat, so it's right. Something unknown and alien to the people around us that we identify, however, is a threat. We're also more likely to believe something if we've been exposed to it before, regardless of how we felt about it then. For example, if someone tells us that the world is flat or that vaccines cause autism, we might brush them off as an oddball. After repeated exposure to these beliefs, however, they begin to curry more favor in our minds, as we come under the impression that many people hold these beliefs, and if lots of people believe in something, we think there must be something to it, because surely that many people can't be wrong about something?

The tendency to fall into this kind of dualistic, black and white thinking is built into our genes. It protects us, physically and emotionally, and leads to a great deal of conflict. It causes us to maintain a rigid stance once we think we're right, leaving us unable to consider other, opposing points of view. We become inflexible and unyielding, completely convinced that our viewpoint is right and that all others are wrong. In reality, however, there is no such thing as being completely right or wrong. Instead of being black and white, these things are in fact many different shades of grey. A person or viewpoint can be right about some things and wrong about others, and opposing viewpoints will have this in common. There are different levels of nuance, complexity, and subtlety built into every point of view and attitude. When we're unable to consider or entertain points of view without outright accepting or rejecting them, we've lost our ability to think critically and make arguments based on their merit and judge them individually, objectively, and impartially. We become entrenched in a particular way of thinking and totally absorbed into a belief without even realizing how narrow-minded we've become. We become unwilling or unable to negotiate or see how both sides can be right and wrong at the same time; this isn't a good state of mind for communication, which involves understanding that there is always more to learn.

Our most difficult and painful emotions are also our most powerful emotions as a result of our evolutionary biology, and for good reason. They're the ones responsible for keeping us alive, right back to the days where we had to run from lions and wolves on grassy plains, and way before. Anger and fear make up a vital part of our fight or flight response, which allows us to stand our ground and fight to the death or run away to save ourselves in dangerous situations. These difficult emotions spark and catalyze conflict when we fail to control them or process them in a healthy way. When someone says or does something that we perceive to be a threat, physically or emotionally, we become defensive. Our emotions are triggered and our response comes out of fear and anger rather than from a reasoned position. When we're in a highly charged emotional state, our choices fall away from us as our reptilian brain takes over from our frontal lobe. We see our options narrow and become increasingly polarized, making it seem like an outburst of aggression is the only choice we have in response to a threat. When we're in this highly charged state, we're like a volcano ready to blow. Our pent up energy and emotions will tend to take the easiest route out; that tends to be through an explosion, rather than through calming down, particularly if we're still in a situation that we perceive on some level to be a threat to us.

This conflict is never productive even when it's in interactions with strangers or people we don't really care about. When it's with our friends and family, however, it can be extremely hurtful. There are few feelings worse than realizing our emotions have gotten the better of us and we've snapped and hurt the people we love most in this world. In order to be able to communicate in spite of conflict stemming from our difficult emotions, we have to be able to process our emotions in a healthy way. We have to accept that they're there and that they will always influence us in order to really begin to live in harmony with them, rather than letting them control and rule us. If we can't manage our feelings and achieve emotional balance, they will manifest themselves in our behavior in ways that lead to and perpetuate conflict.

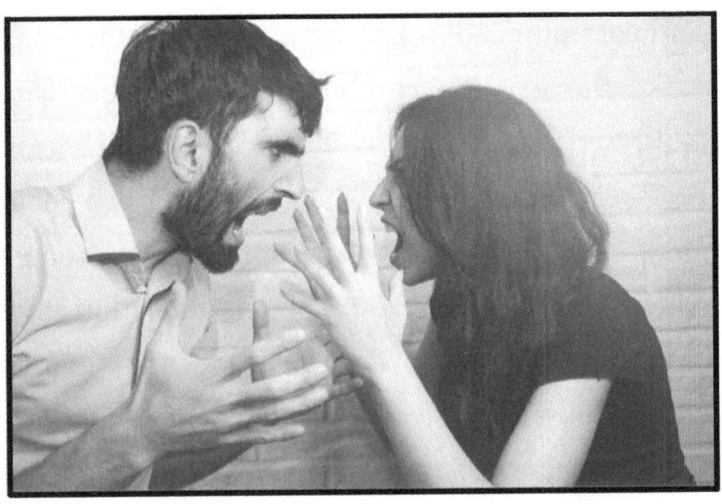

It's worth mentioning here that not everyone is even capable of seeing both sides of an argument at the same time. People suffering from forms of mental illness or personality disorders such as borderline personality disorder, or BPD, have brains that are wired in such a way that balancing and controlling emotion just isn't something they can do in the way other people can. People suffering from these conditions have to work much harder to regulate their emotional life and will have days where they just can't seem to get a grip at all.

Bad communication can both spark conflict and make the existing conflict worse. Conflict can make us less able to communicate, which can lead to vicious cycles where our lack of good communication makes the conflict even worse, which leads to even poorer communication and so on and so forth. When we're highly emotionally charged and involved in a conflict, the last thing we want to do is calm down, sit down, and talk things out in a reasonable way. It almost seems laughable at the time, like a bad joke, because all we want to do is scream and defend ourselves and dominate others and make them see that our views and our own interests are more correct and more important than theirs — because to us, they are.

How to Communicate Through Conflict and Difficult Emotions

Being able to talk and listen in the midst of conflict when the reasoning faculties of your brain are being hijacked by overwhelming emotion is difficult, but it can be done. Positive communication in this context is about trying to remain calm enough to allow your frontal lobe to remain in control of the situation and of your emotions and stopping them from getting the better of you.

Controlling your emotions can be done by focusing on your breathing and on your body, an activity known as meditation. You can both use this is as a tool when you're feeling highly emotionally charged and make it a regular and frequent part of your life. It's a brilliant way to get in touch with yourself and learn how to control your mind and feelings in a positive way. Meditation takes many forms, but one of the most popular and effective types is known as mindfulness meditation. This is a sort of complete focused concentration of your entire conscious awareness and being on your body and your immediate surroundings. It helps to calm and quiet your mind, and focus you on living in the moment, which is known as being 'mindful'.

Here's a step-by-step guide to meditation:

1. **Close your eyes and sit still somewhere comfortable. Try to keep your back straight, it will help you to focus**

2. **Allow your thoughts and feelings to come to you. Don't try to push them away**

3. **Observe your thoughts and feelings, but avoid labeling or judging them**

4. **Bring yourself back to the point of present awareness when you notice yourself becoming distracted by your thoughts**

You may also find that repeating a mantra or phrase to yourself is helpful. This can allow you to focus on the words you're saying and the particular feeling attached to them, rather than the other, more difficult emotions that you're feeling. In order to really gain control of your emotions and learn to balance them, you need to work through your feelings independently and try to work out why it is that you feel the way that you do. The way you feel matters to other people; it's important to realize that this is both because they genuinely care about your mental and emotional wellbeing and the way that you feel directly impacts them through your behavior. Your feelings are worthy. Try to discuss your feelings from your own point of view with the people you feel you can be the most open with, and be solution oriented. You're aiming for emotional balance and regulation.

If you're struggling to communicate through conflict or strong and difficult emotions, you can take a break for as long as you need to allow yourself to calm down before you return to talking about it. There's absolutely no shame in this. Sometimes it's either that or lose your temper completely.

Helping Others to Communicate in Difficult Circumstances

When it comes to what you can do for others to help them to communicate when they're least able to, the most important thing you can do is be patient. You need to give people the time and space to come to terms with the way they feel in their own time and in their own way. If they feel like they're under pressure from you, they will feel even less able to communicate and will withdraw further into their emotions and hostility. Instead, you should show them that you care about them and only want to do what you can to help, and if that means giving them as much time as they need then so be it.

Do your best to keep calm and speak softly. Try not to judge them or yourself. Don't get defensive or take offense to things they might say in the heat of the moment. If you can be open and honest with yourself, it can inspire people to reflect those same principles back to you. You should try to display empathy and the ability to negotiate and consider other, differing points of view. By showing love and kindness and refraining from pushing the person too hard, you let them come to terms with their feelings in their own time. With your encouragement and support, they will come to deal with their emotions in a way that makes sense to them in time. Their emotional communication will improve, and they will develop a greater ability to perceive, facilitate, understand, and manage the way they feel.

Five Steps to Positive Criticism in Relationships

One of the most common causes of conflict within the context of a relationship is critical. No one likes feeling criticized, but being honestly told when you could improve is the driving cause for self-improvement. It's difficult to be impartial or objective about yourself, so we need people to point out when we could do better.

If your partner and you are experiencing consistent conflict in your relationship, it might be because your criticism makes them feel under attack and causes them to get defensive. You can avoid this by following these five steps to positive criticism:

1. **Calm yourself before bringing up a complaint** - When you notice something your partner has done that you believe to be wrong, it's easy to feel annoyed or even angry. This can translate badly and cause resentment and

hostility. Take a few minutes to calm yourself down and get yourself into a mindstate conducive to discussing things. Think about what you want to say, and try to think of a nice memory you have with them before you bring up what you want to say.

2. Use 'I' statements - This can help you to express yourself by talking about things from your point of view, which might help your partner to feel less like they're being attacked by you. Talk about how things make you feel or how they seem to you, rather than speaking about them as though they were objective truth. This can help your partner to put themselves in your shoes as well as being less likely to provoke a defensive reaction.

3. Be specific - Bring up any issues as and when they occur, and talk only about a specific incident. Avoid bringing up things from the past or making sweeping generalizations such as 'you never clean up after yourself' as doing this only makes things worse. This will keep the interaction at a low intensity. It doesn't have to be all doom and gloom, it's just two adults who love and care about each other, helping each other to meet their needs better.

4. Talk about what you need, not what you don't - The point of criticizing in the first place is to help your partner improve. You need to try and make your criticism constructive and creative, rather than using it as an opportunity to pick holes in your partner. tell them how you'd prefer they did something, rather than focusing on what it is that you don't like about what they've done.

5. Above all, be kind - When we feel hurt, it's easy to forget the things that we love about our partner. Our vision narrows to the point where all we can focus on is what's not perfect about them, resulting in us treating them with less kindness and compassion than we'd like to and less than they deserve. Think about how you'd prefer they brought up any issues, and do it that way. Try to show them as much love and kindness as you can. Remember it's about the two of you versus the problem, not you versus them.

Chapter Five: Trust, Honesty, And Respect

After communication itself, trust, honesty, and respect are the most important factors in any relationship, but this is especially true in romantic relationships. These three things form the bedrock of the bond you share with your partner, and without any one of them, a relationship will be unhealthy, toxic, and doomed to failure.

Cultivating Trust in Your Relationship

Genuine trust has to be earned. It has to cut both ways; both partners must be able to trust each other if they're going to make their relationship work. Building trust takes time and effort. Think of it as a savings account; you make small deposits often, and over time your balance grows. It's the same thing with trust. There are a few things you can practice consistently and frequently that will help you to cultivate the trust you share with your partner bit by bit over a long period of time. All you can do is try your best, but with your encouragement and demonstration of the principles you value, your partner will be able to mirror your behavior and help to build your trust in them.

- **Do what you say** - Be a person of your word. How can you expect your partner to trust you if you're not reliable? Personal integrity is extremely important — it's a measure of your character. If your partner can't believe that you take your integrity seriously, they won't be able to trust you.

- **Be honest** - No matter what, you have to be open and honest. If you mess up, make mistakes, or can't stick to your word, then own it. Apologize, explain yourself, and always speak your mind, no matter how hard that might be.

- **Be genuine** - Don't feel like you have to be happy and smiling 24/7. Be yourself, be true to yourself, and don't let yourself feel pressured to pretend to be anyone else. If you're upset, or bored, or annoyed, then own it. Go with it, embrace it. There's nothing worse for a relationship or for yourself than pretending to be somebody you're not. If it's your relationship that's getting you down, don't try to hide it. There are issues there that need to be addressed and pretending you're fine will only kick the can further down the road.

- **Let your partner in** - Building trust is about having intimacy and closeness. It's about you and your partner knowing each other, as well as you, know yourselves. Trust isn't a feeling, but a state of mutual confidence that comes with the close bond of intimacy, of knowing each other inside and out. Letting someone else into your inner emotional life isn't always easy, but even little by little it gets better with time. Once you begin to let them in behind the walls you put up for everyone else, your relationship will truly begin to blossom and flourish.

- **Let it go** - Everybody has baggage, and few people ever really shrug it off and leave it behind. It's easier said than done, but in order to move forward and break new ground, you have to try your very best not to dwell on the past. What's done is done, and it can't be changed. What's important is the present, and that can be as beautiful as you want to make it.

- **Remember that you're both only human** - If you expect perfection from anyone, let alone your partner, you're going to be sorely disappointed. It just isn't possible. Everyone has their flaws. All that you can really ask of your partner is for them to try their best. If their best isn't good enough, that's okay. Some things just aren't meant to be. Try to avoid falling into the trap of criticizing every little flaw you notice in your partner. Being strict and expecting them to live up to impossibly high standards isn't conducive to a healthy and fulfilling relationship.

- **Be prepared to give the benefit of the doubt** - Everybody makes mistakes, and your partner will do too. Cultivating genuine and lasting trust in each other is about being able to give each other the benefit of the doubt when things go wrong and feelings are hurt. Most of the time when we've made mistakes we never wanted anyone to get hurt; it just happens. It's going to happen in your relationship, too, so you have to be prepared to forgive and trust even when they've caused you to doubt them through their actions.

Building a Safe Environment

A sense of emotional and physical safety is essential to the health of any romantic relationship. If both people don't feel safe and secure with the other, their relationship is a toxic one. We need to feel secure around the people we love and spend most of our time with. We need to feel free to be ourselves and to fail and make mistakes and know that it doesn't matter because our partner has our back no matter what. Our relationships should be safe spaces, where we feel totally heard, understood, and supported.

For some people, this can be a difficult concept to understand and put into practice within the context of a relationship. It involves giving the other person the space to be themselves and be free to grow unimpeded. For people that are overly critical and obsessed with their partner being as close to ideal as possible, this isn't something they're good at doing. Their constant attempts to explain exactly what it is about their partner that they don't like and what they would like to be different end up suffocating them; the other partner feels trapped, like there's nothing they can do to please the person they love, and like they will never be good enough to satisfy them.

Having this kind of atmosphere in a relationship is corrosive and toxic. Think of people like plants: they need space and the right nutrients and light to grow. If the conditions aren't right, they will wilt and wither, unable to thrive to their full potential. Relationships are about helping to build each other up, supporting one another, and allowing each other to push on and flourish in every aspect of their lives. A safe, supportive environment is necessary in order for a relationship to be anchored in solid foundations that it can go on to grow and blossom. Such an environment needs predictability and warmth, with the ability to do whatever makes you happy without feeling judged. A relationship should be a place of empathy and loving kindness, where you're free to fail and make mistakes and be less than perfect while being able to grow and learn and pick yourself back up with the loving mutual support and respect from your partner.

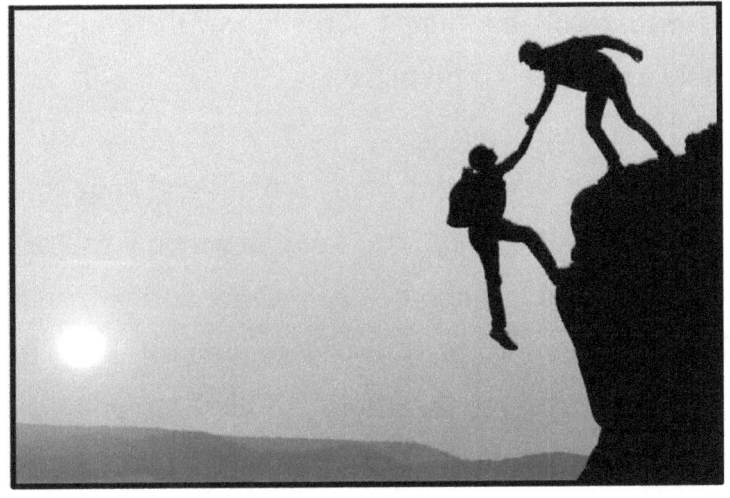

Building an environment like this in your relationship is a matter of looking into yourself, rather than looking at your partner's behavior, and realizing that it takes mutual work from both people in order to make the relationship a safe and secure place. A lot of people feel like their partner is to blame for most or all of the problems in their relationship, which is never the truth of the matter. They feel like they will always be unhappy unless their partner can change, without understanding that they are in control of their own happiness, their own thoughts, feelings, beliefs, and behavior.

You have to take control of yourself and your role in your relationship. You can change how you act towards and feel about your partner and yourself. You can empower yourself and learn how to become happier and more fulfilled all on your own, which can then in turn help to spur your partner on. You can't control your partner; you can't control anyone except yourself, but you can control yourself and inspire and encourage your partner that way. Each of you is responsible for yourselves and for journeying alongside and supporting and encouraging each other, but in order to participate fully in each other's journey and become the excellent partners you could be for each other you need to cooperate fully in thought and in action. You need to be aware of each other's needs and the differences between the two of you. You need to meet each other in the middle and be able to find common ground through a compromise where you can both be happy. You have to be able to take each other's needs into consideration and accommodate any differences in expressing love or communication. If your partner needs more words of praise and love and affirmation that you do, then you must be prepared to say those things more and they must be prepared to accept less than they would like, as long as you're making an effort to work on it.

Repairing Broken Trust

Trust is the lifeblood of a relationship. Once it has been lost, it can be very difficult, if not impossible, to get back. The person who has had their trust broken will find it hard to trust anyone in the same way again, but they will find it especially difficult to ever trust the person who broke it again. Broken trust is one of the most troubling and damaging things that can happen to a relationship. Before it is broken, most people see no reason to doubt their partner or their intentions. They have confidence in them, they have faith in the person they are and they believe that they'd never do anything that could put the relationship they share into jeopardy. When they find out about something that has happened that represents a big breach in trust, then, such as infidelity, it feels as though the person they trusted, the person they thought they knew, is, in fact, someone entirely different, someone who has only been pretending all along.

It's for this reason that the first step in repairing broken trust is that both partners have to acknowledge the reality of their situation. The old relationship is gone; it's dead and buried. Now that people have been hurt and bridges burned, the two of you have a choice to make. You have to decide whether you want to release the relationship and go your separate ways or try to repair things between the two of you by forging a new relationship together that learns from the mistakes you've made in the past. This second option is an incredibly hard process, and it's the reason that major breaches of trust so often represent the death knell for a relationship. Salvaging a relationship from an event as traumatic, complex, and confusing as this requires a total commitment from both parties to explore each other and themselves in depth in order to ask and answer difficult questions and understand all of the factors that have contributed to the current state of the relationship. Both sides have to completely come clean and own their mistakes. There needs to be total, unconditional honesty, emotional transparency, and a real commitment to change and healing.

Understanding, empathy, and patience are needed more than ever, here, on both sides. Both individuals need to feel like they can be completely open without being subject to acts of grievance or revenge. Of course, no one can be asked to not be upset with what they might hear from a partner that's being completely honest and open their heart, but there needs to be a mutual understanding that everything comes out into the open and is dealt with individually without fear of reprisals. I know of many couples where the admittance or discovery of unfaithfulness led to acts of revenge from hurt partners trying to even the score. If you're going to save a relationship, this cannot happen. There needs to be an atmosphere of total forgiveness and healing; a feeling that whatever happens, the worst is behind you. The old relationship is gone, and with it need to go grudges and resentment. This is an incredibly hard thing to do, but if you're going to make it work it has to be done. As difficult as it is, you can't allow yourself to dwell on what has happened. The past has to be left in the past. It can't be brought up every time there's a petty argument or the person that had their trust broken wants to pull an ace out of their boot in order to 'win' a conflict. You talk about everything you need to, you dissect and discuss everything to death in order to learn the important lessons that need to be learned, and then you box it all up, pack it away, and make a commitment to moving on and living for the present and future.

Communication becomes more vital than ever to the relationship at this point. It makes or breaks, so both people need to dig deep and commit to fighting for each other and for the bond they share. you need to communicate openly and with complete honesty; you need to bare your soul to your partner. It can be tempting to not allow yourself to trust a word that comes out of your partner's mouth — after all, they seem like a different person. They could be capable of anything; the person you thought knew and loved wouldn't have been able to do this to you. The hard truth, however, is that the vast majority of the time, a person that greatly breaks the trust in a relationship isn't a psychopath. They're just a person that made a big mistake, or a series of mistakes. Unfortunately, hurting the people that you love is part of the human condition. Everybody makes mistakes, and our hearts and minds can sometimes become so wrapped up and absorbed by something that we lose all sight of the bigger picture, leaving us to come to our senses and realize what a huge mistake we've made only after it's all said and done.

Forgiveness is the single factor that will determine whether or not your relationship can be salvaged once the trust has been lost. In order to truly move on, there needs to be complete and mutual forgiveness of both parties of each other and themselves — not just for the breach of trust, but for all of the hurt both people have caused each other and themselves throughout the entirety of the old relationship. There needs to be a clean slate, a fresh start, a chance to put the past behind you and heal completely. It will take time, however, and there need to be certain new aspects of the relationship that have to be accepted. For example, the person who had their trust broken cannot just be expected to start trusting their partner again. That's not how it works. Once bitten, twice shy. Once the trust is gone, it needs to be built up again, and that will take a lot of time, hard work, and dedication. The partner who had their trust broken often needs complete transparency, including the power to access details of the breaker's personal life, such as their phone and social media accounts. Checking up on the activity and ongoing doubts about trusting come with the territory of having your trust broken, and they need to be embraced if the genuine trust is ever going to have a chance to come back. The victim will need certain assurances if they're going to be able to trust their partner again, and that means total transparency, even at the cost of privacy. That's a privilege of the relationship that gets given up once trust has been broken.

Determining whether or not broken trust can be repaired is largely dependent on the context of the breaking. One-off mistakes, while still awful for the victim, are more forgivable and understandable than repeated lying and a pattern of deceit. The time it takes for the person who messed up to come clean, the nature of the breaking of the trust, and the motivations and reasons for breaking it all come into play here, too. Whatever a couple decides to do at this point, healing needs to take place for both people to go on to live happy and fulfilling lives, regardless of whether that happens together or individually. Healing happens best when a person is able to talk about their feelings to others that are close to them. Being able to confide in someone that you trust and discussing the events that happened to you in the form of a story you tell are important — just make sure that you tell it honestly, and don't allow yourself to become the victim, as that will only create a negative mentality and cause you to feel resentment.

The final piece of the puzzle when it comes to repairing broken trust is learning to be honest with, trust, and respect yourself. This is often overlooked in favor of an emphasis on cultivating these values with the other person in the relationship. However, it is just as important, if not even more important, to make sure that you have an open, honest, and trusting relationship with yourself. Before you can look out and make real, tangible changes in the way you live your life, you have to first learn to look inwards and understand yourself.

Getting Your Partner to Open Up to You

Openness and intimacy are essential ingredients in a healthy and fulfilling relationship. If there is an emotional distance between your partner and you, it can be hard trying to work out how to bridge the gaps and bring the two of you closer together. This usually isn't a case of differing desires, as if the two of you didn't want to be closer, you probably wouldn't be together. More often than not, it simply comes down to a lack of understanding of what is needed to foster emotional closeness in a romantic relationship.

Opening up to another person puts you in a very vulnerable position emotionally. It's as if you're removing the armor you wear to protect yourself from the outside world or bridging the gap you use to keep everybody else at a distance. At the end of the day, no one can hurt you if you don't let them in and give them the power to break your heart. Cultivating openness in a relationship is therefore about facilitating your partner's ability to be vulnerable by being a safe and loving person and creating an atmosphere in your relationship in which they can feel safe and comfortable opening up and revealing their inner emotional being. Doing this is a matter of being a reliably positive, calming, understanding presence for your partner, and showing them that it's safe to open up to you by first doing so yourself. By putting your heart on the line like this and revealing your inner thoughts and feelings, you signal to your partner that they can do the same; you have as much to lose as they do, and you're happy to risk it all the same.

Creating this positive atmosphere and being a calming presence for your partner involves consistently respecting their opinions and feelings whenever they voice them and showing a genuine interest in getting to know them inside and out. It involves being receptive to what they have to say and being able to listen attentively without judgment or condemnation for mistakes they might have made or things they might not like about themselves. Opening yourself up emotionally can be a very hard thing for someone to do, especially if they haven't done it before or they've been badly hurt by being vulnerable in the past. Your role, then, is to accommodate this experience by supporting and encouraging your partner and focusing on learning about how they feel about themselves, while also reassuring them that they don't need to judge themselves and that you have plenty of things you're not so fond of about yourself, too. This openness and receptiveness will over time help to adjust the way your partner feels about themselves and allow them to feel more relaxed about the idea of opening up. Your influence, patience, and acts of kindness, big and small, will help to determine how safe and comfortable your partner feels with you, and therefore the extent to which they can really reveal their inner emotional being.

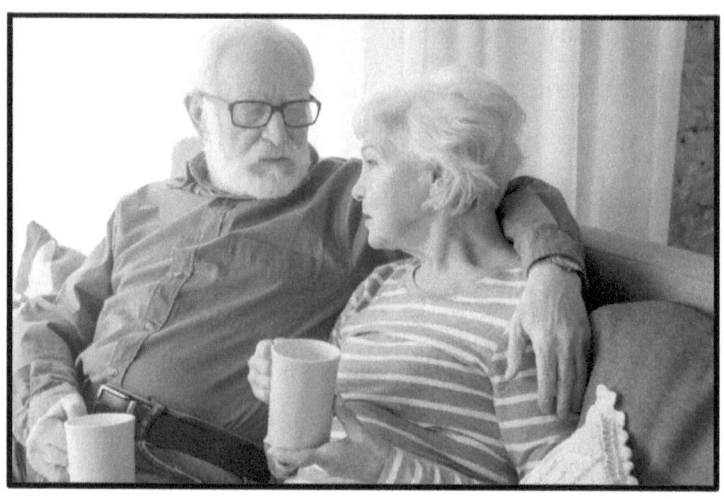

Quick tip: When a person is focused on how they feel about themselves, the predominant emotions they experience tend to be doubtful and questioning, and self-conscious. Part of helping them to open up to you is to share your own inner being with them in order to allow them to focus on how

> you feel about yourself, shifting their focus and helping them to feel more comfortable about the idea of following in your footsteps. If you feel comfortable enough to open up about yourself without fear of being judged then chances are that in time, they will be, too.

Staying in Love

Perhaps the hardest thing to accept about love is that it can never be perfect. I'm sure that all of us at one point or another in our lives have experienced that longing for perfect love, for our soulmate, who we'd lock eyes with and fall head over heels for and then live happily ever after with, without any of the difficulty or hard times that come with our experiences of love in reality. The thing is, nothing and no one is perfect. There is no such thing as a truly fairy-tale ending. There are several different stages of maturity in love that people go through, with different levels of understanding of each other and the relationship in each.

- **Phase One: Yearning** - This stage represents the beginning of a new relationship. It's often referred to as the 'honeymoon' period and is characterized by fireworks, passion, and infatuation. It has low clarity, however; neither partner has even begun to scratch the surface of the other, and so there is a low clarity about the relationship and a lack of understanding of what being together would actually look like. Even though the relationship at this stage is completely untested and both people are essentially strangers to each other, the intensity of 'love' chemicals in the brain commonly make both individuals feel like they could be together forever.

- **Phase Two: Earning** - The second stage of a relationship kicks in once the honeymoon period comes to an end. This phase is characterized by a decrease in the number of love-generating chemicals and hormones in the brain, leading to a feeling of lowered intensity and even a frostiness or pulling away in feeling as compared to the first stage. The clarity of both partners as to the content of the relationship and of each other's character becomes much clearer as they learn about each other. The commitment of each person at this point comes into question as they come face to face with reality.

- **Phase Three: Enduring** - This is the final stage in the maturation of a relationship. At this point, the love-generating chemicals in the brain cease to become relevant, and the flame of passion burns down into a smoldering, glowing heat. At this point, the clarity of both people as to the nature of the relationship becomes crystal clear, and their commitment stable, enduring, and lasting. Even once the relationship has reached this stage, the passion can be re-ignited from time to time, as though stoking the fire and adding more fuel through finding new ways to bond and explore each other and life more deeply. The flame of love might smolder, but it only goes out if you let it go out.

Being in a committed, long term relationship instead involves putting in the effort to keeping the love alive. Love is a choice and an action, rather than a feeling. it's a way of treating your partner and having a certain attitude towards the relationship you have with them. Understanding the true nature of relationships and the shifts that they naturally go through can make it easier to adjust when they happen to you. Keeping a relationship alive and lasting is about assuming a positive position on it and striving to put in the effort to make it work. You have to almost treat it as though you never stop dating, continuously striving to do nice and thoughtful things for each other just because you want to make each other happy.

Even if you feel negative about your relationship, this can be an incredibly powerful realization. Your relationship is what it is. No matter who you're with, it can always be better and it can always be worse. It's all about the way you look at things. The fact of the matter is, you're still with them, and if you take on a positive attitude the only way to go is up. It's always better to assume the position of 'my relationship is good' and then work to improve it, rather than looking for ways to drag it down, pick holes, and find flaws in it.

Lots of people fall into the trap of getting hooked on the passion and endorphins of the honeymoon stage of a new relationship and then bounce from partner to partner, falling head over heels again and again before growing bored, constantly searching for 'the one' who they won't ever feel their love slip away from after just a handful of months. This mentality just isn't realistic, and will only leave you with a lifetime of regret at missed opportunities with people who you could have made it work with and had a beautiful and fulfilling relationship if only you'd had the understanding that a perfect love just isn't possible to find.

A part of the fact that love is a choice that you make is that it's an active experience, rather than passive. You get out what you put in, and the more you feed into it and nourish it the more it will be sustained. It needs to be cared for and cultivated like you would a garden. If the right conditions aren't met or the proper care isn't provided, a relationship can end up neglected and starved. There are five areas in particular that need to be focused on in order to keep the bond between yourself and your partner fulfilling:

1. **Safety** - you have to make your partner feel safe and secure with you and in the relationship. This includes trust and openness with you.

2. **Appreciation** - You have to show your gratitude to your partner for their presence in your life, emotional support, and friendship that they provide for you, and the fact that they stick by you. It's important to validate your partner and acknowledge their feelings.

3. Respect - This is essentially being nice to your partner and considerate of their needs. It involves keeping their confidence, and not selling them out or betraying them in any way. It also includes a consideration of their opinions and consulting with them before making any decisions that would affect both of you.

4. Encouragement and support - Being a good partner to your significant other is about building them up and supporting them through thick and thin. They'll need your encouragement and your advice and help through all of the best and worst moments of their life.

5. Dedication - This could also be seen as effort, and is one of the most influential factors in keeping your love alive as it determines how much work you are willing to put into your relationship. Without dedication and effort from both parties, a relationship will slowly grind to a halt and end with a whimper as both people wonder why it's even worth trying and go their separate ways.

> **Quick tip:** Every interaction that you have with your partner will either be positive or negative. It will either be one of love, energy, and attentiveness, or of apathy and disinterest and even spite. In this way, the bedrock and character of your relationship are constructed in the present, with the actions you do and the attitude you take, each and every moment. It's built out of the texts and the phone calls and the small acts of loving kindness and thoughtfulness. You can bring a certain inspiration, constructive creativity and positive energy to your relationship, or you can be destructive through neglect or malice, and let it crumble and erode away. Your choices are your own, and your relationship is what you make it. You can intentionally change your attitude towards your relationship to bring

> better energy to it, and treat your partner as the person you love and cherish. This way, you can keep your relationship alive and stop the two of you from falling out of love.

Chapter Six: Relationship Killers

In this section, we'll be looking at the things that can kill relationships off, whether it's short and sharp or long and drawn out and full of suffering.

Self-Destructive Behavior

Any relationship is about a bond between two people. When the relationship is sufficiently close, events and circumstances in the life of one half of the relationship will have an impact on the other. This is the reason why self-destructive behavior can be so instrumental in ending relationships; when one person is set on a downward spiral, the people around them will jump ship at some point in order to avoid being sucked into the whirlpool of negativity that the self-destructive person represents. Self-destructive behavior causes the destruction of relationships wherever it occurs, and it often leads to us hurting the ones we love the most.

The range of self-destructive behavior is wide and varied. In essence, it's any behavior that ends up bringing negative results to the person perpetrating it, whether or not they intend it to. It also includes those attitudes and state of mind that inevitably leads to negative and destructive consequences for people. Some of the most common and debilitating examples of self-destructive behavior include:

- **Criticism (whether intentional or not)**
- **Disrespect**
- **Laziness**
- **Having to be right**
- **Nastiness and spite**

- **Negativity**
- **Substance abuse**
- **Selfishness**
- **Assuming the worst**
- **Digging up the past**
- **Failing to take responsibility for your own actions / blaming others or the world for your problems**
- **Being obsessed with punishment**
- **Grudges and resentment**
- **Arrogance**
- **Digging up the past**
- **Always thinking the grass is greener somewhere else**
- **Compulsive Lying**

Self-destructive behavior is less about individual behaviors than it is about the attitude a person has towards themselves and the people around them. When a person is self-destructive, they tend to reflect several or more of these attributes in a pattern of negativity and toxicity that has real consequences for their own lives and for the people they know and have relationships with. The net effect of being a person who is overly critical, selfish, lazy, arrogant, and always has to be right is that nobody wants to know them because they're obnoxious and bring everybody else down. The same goes for people who are always negative and assume the worst about everyone and everything, or people who hold grudges and are obsessed with getting their own back. The effect is the same; they drive everybody away from them and end up killing relationships.

When a person exemplifies these behaviors and attitudes, they're hurting themselves more than anyone else. The negativity, the toxicity, and the bitterness that radiates out of them come from a place of deep hurt but is poisoning them in exactly the same way it's poisoning all of the relationships in their life. Changing these harmful behaviors involves a person changing their mind-state and attitude. This piece of advice is commonly offered and even more commonly brushed off as nonsense, because surely if becoming a happier and more pleasant person was as simple as thinking positively then it would be easy to do, right? Wrong. It's simple, but that doesn't mean it's easy. Changing a sequence of self-destructive behaviors means a person totally overhauling their personality and the type of energy that they bring to themselves and the circumstances of their life in favor of a different way of seeing themselves and the world around them.

This can be a difficult enough task even with therapy and counseling, but it can be done by a person all by themselves. All that is required is a desire to change for the better, to become a better, more positive person. Once this desire is alight in a person's heart, they will be capable of pulling themselves out of the negative, bitter slump they're in, eventually allowing them to see life with a totally new perspective. To do this, such a person must first do some soul searching. They have to look in the mirror and ask themselves what they want to do with the opportunity they've been given in the form of life. What do they want their legacy to be, for themselves and for the people they know? Do they want to spend their days bitter at the world and being a toxic influence on the people they meet, or do they want to enjoy their lives and focus on being a positive and pleasant person, who creates value for other people and makes their lives and the world that little bit better of an experience?

Once this desire is present in a person, they can go on to make great strides of improvement, first to the way they view themselves and then to the way they view the other people in their life. What's needed here is an appreciation for the good things in life, a sense of gratitude for the beautiful experiences we can have and the incredible people we can meet. It requires a thirst for seeing the good there is in the world, as well as the bad, and making a conscious decision to focus their attention and energy on the positive rather than the negative. From there, negative and self-destructive attributes can be replaced with positive and constructive ones. Selfishness can be replaced with selflessness, with acting in order to help and assist others rather than in worrying about themselves. Arrogance can be replaced with humility, with the knowledge that no one is flawless and that everyone makes mistakes. Resentment can be replaced with forgiveness, with moving on to live and let live. The negative things we hold on to bring us down far more than anyone else - which is precisely why they're so self-destructive.

A big part of what makes positive change so hard, especially after you've lived with a negative and bitter mindset for so long, is that changing means having to admit to yourself and by proxy the wider world that you were wrong for so long; that your negativity and bitterness were misplaced, and that ultimately, it was your choice to live that way, rather than it being a burden you're forced to carry as a result of the events of your life and the nature of the world. Taking responsibility for all of this is an incredibly difficult and painful thing to do, and is often the reason why some people come close to making a positive change in their lives, only to dig their heels in harder and double down in their misery at the last hurdle. Confronting the reality of our lives being directed far more by the way we react to events than it is about the events that happen to us is horrible, but it's necessary in order to begin to really start living well. We're often blind to things until they're revealed to us in such a way that the penny finally drops and everything makes sense. Sometimes we need to experience things directly in order to truly understand them, and until then, we can only do the best we can with what we have at any one time, even if those things aren't for the best for us or anyone else; we often think that we have no choice but to do them.

Codependency

Co-dependency is an interesting and complex concept that gives us a fascinating glimpse into human psychology. It's a bit like quicksand; once you're in, you're stuck, and the harder you fight to free yourself the deeper you get sucked in. It's a behavioral condition in relationships where one person enables another's mental illness, addiction, immaturity, or irresponsibility. It can happen in any kind of relationship dynamic, commonly manifesting itself as a person's total reliance on romantic partners, siblings, parents, friends, and co-workers. It's also sometimes known as 'relationship addiction' because people with codependency tend to feel a great need to form one-sided, emotionally abusive, and shallow relationships with people that they can then manipulate to provide for their needs. A codependent person will go to great lengths to ensnare and trap people that they can lean on heavily in order to sustain their mental or behavioral issues while having someone to take care of them and make sure that their needs are met.

It's commonly seen in cases of severe drug addiction, such as alcoholism, although it also often crops up in people with mental and chronic physical illness. It's a total reliance on someone else, with the codependent person refusing to do anything to look after themselves or stand on their own two feet, independently. People with codependency have to find a person that will look after them, a process known as 'enabling'. This enabling sustains the codependent person's negative behavior and allows them to continue in their lifestyle. People drawn to this enabling role tend to be close friends and family of the codependent family, and are usually people that feel an amount of satisfaction by being the hero and savior of a person in need. By 'rescuing' the codependent person in the form of providing resources and support, enablers may feel that they're doing the right thing regardless of how it affects their own life. The truth, however, is that all they're doing is allowing an ill person to persist in their illness without getting the appropriate help and learning how to become independent.

Not all enablers are willing participants in the codependent relationship, however. Codependent people are good manipulators and can go to extreme lengths in order to guilt-trip and otherwise persuade people into looking after them and becoming their enabler. They wield emotionally abusive tactics like gaslighting in order to tighten their grip on the person they're trying to get to enable their behavior, which can over time cause that person to really believe that the codependent person simply cannot manage without them. Codependency is a learned behavior, often being passed down through dysfunctional families where younger members of the family observe how older members ensure that their needs are met in order to sustain their addictions or negative behavior and repeat the pattern themselves.

Breaking codependent habits and becoming more independent isn't something that a person with this condition can do while they're being enabled. The cycle needs to be broken the enabler or enablers in their life refraining from rescuing them. It's only by forcing the codependent person to have to take care of themselves that the negative or addictive behavior can be stopped. This can be difficult, however, as they often make a compelling argument in order to persuade people to continue to take care of them. Their enablers soon become trapped, with the grip of the codependent person tightening and making it harder to escape. Relationships with codependent people are always dysfunctional due to the nature of their condition; they seep others as means to an end, rather than having a healthy outlook on the people they know. This makes maintaining any kind of relationship with codependent people incredibly difficult, resulting in bridges being burned and relationships being killed off over the years.

Control Freaks

People that feel an excessive need to be in control tend to drive away those closest to them because of their rigid inability to tolerate uncertainty. The very nature of life is uncertain; you can't control anything in life apart from the way you react to things that happen to you — your own attitude and behavior. This means that control freaks are fighting a losing battle, and the side effects of this manifest themselves as toxic behavior as they desperately try to order and control all of the things in their life.

There's a good reason why some people seek to exercise control over the circumstances of their life and the people they know. In a sense, control is freedom; it's the freedom to choose what happens. We want control over our lives in order to choose what happens to us and direct ourselves to a certain place where we think we'll be happy. The problem is that other people's freedom tends to impinge on our own, and this is where control battles come into play. Control freaks can only control their lives to the extent that they can control the people within it, and so they're constantly trying to shape and mold others into being what *they* want them to be, rather than respecting the right of individuals to be independent and make their own choices.

Controlling relationships can happen anywhere, but they most commonly crop up in dynamics where the controlling person naturally has a great deal of control over another, such as parents or romantic partners, and it is, therefore, less of a stretch to control more and more of a person's life as they're already closely linked. Because people tend to be naturally independent, the behavior of control freaks only makes the people in their life pull further away from them in an attempt to avoid being caught up in the way the control freak wants everything in their life to be ordered. This means that controlling behavior often only ends one way — with breakups, friends pulling away, and children getting out of the family home as soon as they can in order to live their own lives on their own terms.

Becoming a less controlling person is about coming to not only tolerate but appreciate the uncertainty and chaos that are the natural state of life. Rather than seeking to have everything run according to their expectations, the controlling person must come to understand that all they can really control is the way they react to life and that the beauty and enjoyment in life come from going with the flow rather than trying to swim against the current. People have the right to self-determination, and they will do what they will. There's no way to prevent people from hurting you, either. If someone is going to hurt or betray you, then it's going to happen, and there's nothing that can be done to prevent or control it.

Insecurity

Everyone feels insecure from time to time, but when it becomes a defining part of our everyday life, insecurity can become very troublesome for our own self-esteem and the relationships we have with other people in our lives, with whom we're constantly second-guessing the opinions and thoughts of and seeking reassurance and validation from. Although insecurity can affect all kinds of relationships, it is at its most destructive in romantic ones, where so much of ourselves and our own identity is placed in the bond we have with another person and questions surrounding what they truly think about us, whether or not we're good enough for them, if they think we're good enough, if we're smart enough or good looking enough and whether they accept us or not all come bubbling to the surface in spates of anxiety and worry. This need for other people's approval undermines our confidence and trust in ourselves, pulling us further and further away from feeling happy in our own bodies and minds and towards needing constant validation and acceptance from other people in order to maintain a feeling of self-worth.

This problem has been exacerbated significantly in the age of social media, where we can upload pictures of ourselves in order to receive quantifiable feedback about how loved or admired or appreciated we are from the people we know. We all want to feel secure and confident, and often we don't. It's the nature of life. When this issue gets out of hand, though, it can turn us into a black hole, sucking in reassurance and validation of others at ever increasing rates, trying to fill a void inside of us that can never be filled by the acceptance and love of anyone other than ourselves. This can be especially problematic when it comes to our partners and significant others, as the insecurity that causes us to fall in upon ourselves can take hold of them and bring them down with us. Our unquenchable thirst for their approval and reassurance can lead to them feeling drained and as though they're not enough for us, which in a sense, they aren't. No one can ever be enough for an insecure person. No amount of outside approval and validation will ever fill the void they feel deep inside. Only their own love and approval and acceptance will be able to heal this wound.

Overcoming insecurity, first of all, requires an understanding of why we feel insecure. It's okay to be insecure, but we have to figure out where it's coming from in order to fix it. The self-consciousness and doubt we feel towards ourselves when we're insecure ultimately stems from our focus on how other people feel about us and how we feel about ourselves. We're totally absorbed by and tied up with ourselves; with the way we're perceived by others and by ourselves. This causes us a great deal of anxiety because we're constantly worrying about how we appear to other people and what they think about us. In reality, it doesn't matter what anyone thinks about you. All that is important is how you feel about yourself.

Although it might seem counterintuitive, becoming more comfortable with ourselves requires getting out of our own way and realizing that how we feel about ourselves or how other people perceive us is irrelevant. Instead, we can focus on how others perceive themselves in order to distract us from constantly second-guessing ourselves and worrying about how we appear. We can use 'metacognition' or think about thinking, to learn about how our minds process our relationship with ourselves. We can then notice that we have a much higher level of choice and control over how we feel about ourselves than we might have previously thought. We become more confident in ourselves and comfortable in our own skin when we realize that we are good enough, that we have always been good enough because we are who we are and that's okay, no matter who we are.

> **Quick tip:** We have to embrace all of the things that make us unique, both good and bad. We have to accept our flaws and realize that everybody else is just as flawed and just as capable of being a villain as we are. It's only when we come to the understanding that everyone feels insecure and doubts themselves sometimes that we realize we have to love and accept ourselves first and foremost. We can express gratitude for our lives and the opportunity we have by focusing on how others feel about themselves, rather than on how they feel about us or how we feel about ourselves.

Fixing a Broken Relationship

Romantic relationships are incredibly confusing and complicated. Navigating them is one of the hardest things we have to do in our lives. In order to heal rifts and fix a relationship, the first step is to find out what exactly it is that's broken. Just like taking a car to the mechanic or going to the doctor, you have to make a diagnosis before you can begin taking steps to address and solve the problem. This is where the majority of couples get in trouble when it comes to trying to fix issues in their relationship — they can't figure out where the real problem lies because they get bogged down on blaming each other and worrying about who is right or wrong. In reality, no one is right and no one is wrong. When there are issues in a relationship, the blame is always shared. Working out who is right and who is wrong isn't important; making a diagnosis is.

In order to fix a relationship, you first have to take a step back and realize that the two of you are a team. The mentality you need to have as a couple in order to overcome obstacles is that it's the two of you versus the problem. Trying to work out who's right and who's wrong and placing the blame on each other only separates you and pushes you further apart when what you really need is to make a stand together and use teamwork and mutual support to figure out the problems and tackle them as a unit. You have to set your ego aside and embrace the idea of working together in order to float rather than stepping on each other trying to grasp for air. If you take the latter approach, the relationship will drown. You are entitled to feel however you want to feel, but if you really want to make things work, you have to commit to being a team.

Communication is key. Commit to the journey of life together, to continue learning about each other and pushing the depths of your understanding deeper and further. Talk to each other, be open and honest, and give each other the time and space to really hear each other out.

If you want to make things work, then love hasn't been lost. Sometimes it just takes a different way of seeing things in order to rediscover all the incredible things that you've come to take for granted in each other. Life is short, so try not to take things too seriously. Try to lighten up, enjoy each other's company and have some fun. Be nice to each other, and remember that no matter what happens, you're in it together.

Chapter Seven: Ending Relationships

Part of being a good communicator and understanding relationships involves knowing how to bring them to a close in a positive way when it's time to call it a day. In this section, we'll be looking at how to do exactly that.

Breaking Up in the Right Way

The reality of life is that many relationships have to come to an end sooner or later. We can't all be with the first person we date forever. Communication is as essential in ending relationships as it is in maintaining them. The way in which we break up with our partners directly determines the amount of suffering and heartache that they feel. When we handle things maturely and respectfully through the good use of communication skills, we can keep the agony our partner feels at being broken up with to a minimum.

- **Make sure you're certain** - Once you play the breakup card, you can't take it back. Breaking up is now on the table, and even if you decide that you've made a mistake and you want to be together, after all, it won't come off. The first fight or disagreement will only drag everything back up again. If you're not certain about what you want to do, then wait and do nothing until you're totally sure of how you feel. You can't afford to make any rash decisions with so much at stake.

- **Once you've made up your mind, end things quickly** - When you know what you want and need to do, do it as soon as possible. You have to make a sharp break. Life is desperately short, so you have to do what's right for both of you. It's not fair on you or them to go on if you're not happy with the way things are. If you've got plans made such as a holiday booked or a birthday you've bought a present for, you'll need to be brave. Those things don't matter in the long run, and you'll feel extremely strange the whole time if you know you're just biding your time until you break up with them. There's never a perfect time to break up, so do it quickly.

- **Don't be unfair** - Clumsy lovers sometimes can't bring themselves to be the bad guy by ending a relationship that they don't want to be a part of anymore, so they do something to force their partner's hand like starting to drink a lot or cheat. Don't be unfair, and don't make things any harder or more painful than they have to be.

- **Do it in person** - You owe your partner enough to be able to break up with them face to face. Spare them the added pain and humiliation of being broken with over the phone or through text.

- **Tell them the facts, keep it specific -** You don't need to be nasty about it by bringing up every tiny flaw and minor detail you've ever disliked about them. What you do have to do is lay out the facts of why you're breaking up with them as clearly as you can, keeping it specific and sticking to the basic information. Explain how you're not right for each other, and admit the wrongs and difficulties that you bring to the relationship to help them to see that it's for the best for both of you if you go your separate ways.

- **Be brave** - You're probably going to be hated by your partner and possibly their friends and family for a while after you call it quits, so be courageous and hang in there. You're doing the right thing if you no longer want to be with them, so don't worry about justifying it to anyone other than yourself.

- **Put yourself in their shoes** - Be as emotionally mature as you can and handle things with tact. Your partner is going to be experiencing a great deal of pain and sadness. They're going to feel the sorrow of losing someone they liked and loved. We often only think about ourselves and how we're gonna take things like this, but it's important for us to put ourselves in their shoes and think about how they're going to feel and what the best way of doing things is before we pull the trigger.

- **Prepare yourself emotionally** - The longer you spend with someone, the more of your life will look strange and weird in retrospect after you break up with them. You'll find you're no longer sure how to feel about all of the memories and souvenirs you have from the relationship, but you have to keep in mind that just because things didn't work out, in the long run, doesn't make the time you spent with them wasted. Be glad that you had the opportunity to make those memories and have those experiences. Regardless of whether or not you feel relieved once you've ended things, you're going to feel horrible afterward. Relationships are a habit, so you'll feel an element of withdrawal once it's over. You'll also lose a lot of emotional support, which can be difficult to process. Take the time to prepare yourself, and hang out with your friends and family to help get you through it.

- **Be committed** - Once you've broken up, go 'no contact'. Let them and yourself heal by distancing yourself. Don't flip flop on your decision. Breaking up is hard enough, so you owe it to the person you've been with for however long to try and break the news to them in a way that is respectful without dangling the thread and giving them hope for a future between the two of you if none exists.

Staying Friends

Whether or not you can stay friends with your ex after the two of you break up depends on the context of your relationship and the manner of your breakup. If you ended things on good terms, with mutual understanding and respect, the odds are better for you to have to maintain a positive friendship with them than if it ends with hostility. Remaining friends after a breakup is difficult, however, as the relationship has been forever changed. It's very hard, if not impossible to be close friends — it's weird going from being so close and intimate to a step down from that. You might find that you begin to feel things that you don't want to feel for them. Being on friendly but more distant terms is far more pragmatic. It's highly dependent on how willing both of you are to stay in touch and to what extent you want to remain a part of each other's lives. Maybe it will work, and maybe it won't. All you can do is wait and see what happens.

If the breakup was a divorce or you have children together, things can be more complicated. You might have to remain on friendly terms for the sake of your kids, or in order to get through the divorce proceedings with the minimum amount of hassle possible. At the end of the day, you can't control hey they feel or what they want to do, so all you can do is look after yourself and enjoy a rich and full life on your own. That way, you're in a position to have that relationship with them if it turns out to be an option, but if not, it's not the end of the world. It's important to be financially independent and completely self-reliant if you have children so that you're not dependent on child support and whatever you do get is a bonus, rather than simply being what is expected. Whatever happens, go forward with your head held high and know that no matter what, life is what you make it. Partners come and go, and although you'll miss them at first, if they're no longer with you, it's for a reason.

Final Words

Communication is one of those skills that everyone possesses but few know how to truly use. Not many people even understand the true potential that communication has to change lives and revolutionize the way you feel about yourself and others. It is the key to living in a way that is successful and fulfilling, and with this book, you've gained the knowledge and the tools to implement it properly in every area and aspect of your life. You've learned about the differences between men and women in terms of how communication is understood and processed, and how to take these differences into account when you communicate. You've learned about how to implement positive communication, how to read body language in order to properly understand the message someone is putting across, and how to make a great first impression on someone every time through the focus of your communication with them.

We've gone over how to communicate and manage relationships at work, as well as how to manage conflict, deal with difficult, negative, and toxic people, and how to know when it's time to remove these people from your life. As social animals, being able to talk to each other and interact is the primary ether through which we construct our lives. Communication makes up the basis of our societies and our individual lives, and the people we share our experiences with are the true determinators of what kind of experience we have in this world. Being able to sustain healthy and balanced relationships with the people we know is therefore essential to being a happy and well-rounded person surrounded by people that uplift and inspire us and who we encourage and support as much as we can. Relationships are mutual, shared experiences, and improving them will help to improve both your lives in a way that you never could have imagined before.

It's my hope that this book has been able to coach you through taking a more proactive and understanding approach to the most important relationships in your life. I hope it has enabled you to better understand the importance of trust, honesty, and respect in forming and maintaining relationships with the people in your life, as well as allowing you to gain a clearer view of those traits and behaviors that can bring relationships to a short, sharp end. Learning all of these things will not only help you to become a better communicator and master of relationships, but also to become a happier, more confident, and deeply fulfilled person.

This book has shown you how to incorporate a more thoughtful and measured approach to communication in every area of your life and will enable you to form and maintain lasting bonds with the great people you meet and sustain and nourish the relationships that you have with the people you love. Life is a minefield, so with this book, I've done my best to communicate the importance and gravity of practicing patience and understanding when it comes to communicating with the people in your life. Everyone is fighting their own internal battles, so having the ability to step back and be impartial in order to deliver a measured and thoughtful response puts you in the very top percentile of communicators on the planet. With the skills you've learned here, you're now ready to get out there and revolutionize the approach you take to communicating with the people you know in a more positive and beneficial way. You'll be able to tackle and handle relationships no matter the context and work out how to get yourself through sticky situations. You'll be able to change your relationship with your partner, friends, and family for the better, and more easily understand why the people in your life do and say the things they do. This ability can be incredibly useful in the weary journey through complex relationships and difficult circumstances that we all face. It will provide clarity and indicate to you the right course of action where before you would have been stumped. Embrace your life and the people in it, and remember that happiness is always best when it's shared.

Life is short, so at the end of the day, all you can do is try your best and surround yourself with good people. When this isn't possible, this book has shown you the way to manage relationships in order to bring those that have run their course to a close and allow you to move ahead towards a brighter, more positive future with the people in your life that uplift and support you, rather than with negative and toxic people who are on a downward path and are only concerned with bringing you down with them. Cut those people loose wherever you can — your life can only improve without them — and remember that you're shaped and defined by the people that you spend the most time with. Spend time with the right people, with positive and encouraging people, and let those who will make your life worse drift away.

I hope you've enjoyed reading it as much as I enjoyed writing it, and that the lessons it has taught you are as beneficial and essential to changing your life for the better as they have been for mine. Remember that your life is in your hands and the relationships you have are completely within your control. All it takes is the desire to shape your life for the better and the know-how that this book has provided you with. Be kind, be brave, and remember to be patient and understanding as much as you can. Communication is as much about really understanding the background around how people's minds work and the reasons they do what they do as it is the raw essence of getting a message across. If you can give people the time and space they need, they'll be able to tell you what they want you to know in their own time.

Good luck!

Book 2: Communication In The Workplace

Everything You Need To Know About Effective Communication Strategies At Work To Be A Better Leader

Introduction

Communication is at the core of every human relationship. We all communicate with each other in some form or another, every day. Communication in the workplace can be especially tricky. The way in which you communicate with other individuals in your workplace or your business, can go a long way in how others perceive you and thus relate to you. Learning to effectively communicate isn't just about resolving conflict in the workplace. Effective communication also plays a large contributing factor in your relationships with clients, the business's profitability, employee engagement and retention and how effectively a team can function together.

Effective communication is a skill that each one of us has the power to master. As an employee, you should make an effort to learn how to effectively communicate, not just for others' benefit, but for yourself as well. In this book you will learn proven strategies on how to effectively communicate with your coworkers or employees and be able to express your message without any confusion or frustration. Successful businesses are built on healthy working relationships and effective communication. As an employee or business owner, you have the power to contribute to the success of the business by honing your communication skills (Bosworth, 2019). Your own personal communication style has an influence on other individuals and can be used to create thriving business relationships. Effective communication in the workplace isn't just about being able to accurately express your ideas or about getting your point across, it is so much more than that. It also goes far beyond just resolving conflict or creating a positive team environment. Being able to effectively communicate in the workplace is essential to client relationships, the company's culture, your sales process, building a better team environment and employee engagement. Building an effective communication strategy within the workplace promotes innovation, removes cultural barriers, helps to mitigate conflict and creates transparency, which helps to promote inclusivity.

But why should you listen to anything I have to say about mastering effective communication in the workplace?

Hi, my name is Shirley Cole and I am a professional management and communications consultant. Over the years, I have helped many executives and organizations achieve a greater impact by teaching them how to focus on the needs of their employees through understanding their communication channels. In addition to this, I also give lectures and seminars all over the world to global organizations which focus on creating solutions for communication problems within team settings. I take great joy in helping to transform organizations using the principles I have outlined in this book.

A lack of effective communication in the workplace can cause a lot of different issues. Someone might drop the ball on an important client project due to a miscommunication. Team members might butt heads due to ineffective communication or employees may not fully understand the company culture. When you can effectively communicate with your team members and coworkers, all of these issues can be avoided.

There is a common thread that I see when I work with organizations, no matter the size or type of industry. The company's workforce is very competent and hard-working, however, they often carry around pervasive bad communication habits which lead to drama, anger, mistrust and low morale. This can happen within that individual team and carry over into other departments. It is my goal in this book to share my vast knowledge on how to overcome personality and communication issues so that you (as an employee or employer) can work towards creating a more comfortable and productive working environment. My clients regularly praise me for positively changing their work processes and helping them to create connections that are authentic, energizing and rewarding with both their colleagues and customers through skillful conversations.

The purpose of this book is to show you how to improve your workplace relations by using effective communication strategies. This can easily be done by learning your coworkers' language of appreciation. By outlining exactly how to effectively communicate authentic messages of appreciation and encouragement to employees, coworkers and leaders; this book will provide you with the tools to create a more positive workplace, improve staff morale and increase employee engagement. Many issues within the workplace stem from the question of how to make people feel appreciated. This comprehensive guide to interpersonal communication will provide you with the tools to do just that, by creating a better environment for production, thriving client relationships, high employee engagement and continual team development.

Here is just a small snapshot of the workplace communication strategies that I have included in this book:

- The psychology behind being able to effectively communicate at work.
- How to become a better listener in the workplace.
- The barriers to effective communication in the workplace and how to overcome them.
- Clarifying your values, finding your voice, and effective goal setting.
- How to correctly give and receive criticism.
- The importance of positivity in the workplace.
- Common communication mistakes

and how to avoid them.
- How to deal with difficult people or bosses.
- Becoming a master at public speaking.
- Managing difficult conversations and time wasters.
- Asking questions that get results.
- Effective communication using body language, verbal and non-verbal skills.

You could try and piece this all together yourself by reading websites and other books that only give you bits and pieces. However, do you really have the time for all that? This is the most comprehensive book that you will find that will give you the exact tools you need in order to create a thriving work environment where everyone appreciates and actually understands one another.

Don't wait for a lack of communication to cripple your client relationships or misunderstandings to muddle your sales process. Whether you work in a cubicle, a factory or within a virtual team, learning effective communication strategies will make a world of difference in your professional life. If you want to create crystal clear workplace communication processes, then keep reading!

Chapter One: The Incredible Power of Effective Communication in The Workplace

So often in the workplace, we send quick emails and memos to one another in order to communicate (sometimes very vital) information. However, there is a major disadvantage to this. Messages can be misinterpreted or misunderstood, which then causes a breakdown in the communication processes. The sole use of technology - such as emails or instant messaging - when communicating within the workplace removes essential information that can be gained through the use of body language and tone of voice.

What Is Effective Communication In The Workplace?

Being able to effectively communicate within the workplace takes place through a series of verbal and non-verbal processes to promote professional relationships. In order to promote effective communication within the workplace, you must first take a look at and identify any potential barriers before moving on.

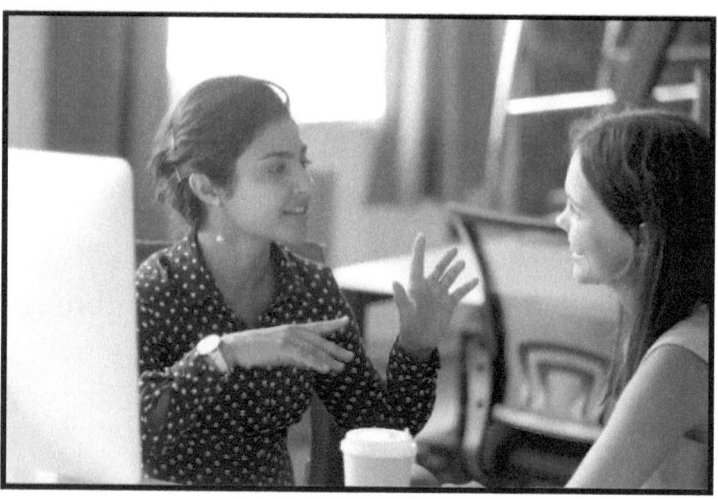

There are many, many barriers to effective communication in the workplace. Some of the most common include interrupting others or interruptions from others, inattentive listening, a failure to properly read body language and other non-verbal cues, gender differences (yes, men and women communicate differently), not getting the whole story or jumping to conclusions and inappropriate reactions (both verbally and non-verbally) to others (Effectivecommunicationadvice.com, 2019). In order to be a more effective communicator in the workplace, there are several things that you can do:

- Ensure that your body language and what you are saying match up.
- Being aware of gender differences in communication styles and how to effectively handle them.
- Having an understanding of cultural differences and how to work with many different types of people.
- Not relying so much on technology and communicating in person.
- Be able to give and receive

constructive criticism
- Keeping emotions out of the equation.

When you work to create effective communication within the workplace it creates positivity and an enjoyable environment for you and those around you. This can also help to decrease workplace stress while increasing productivity and overall employee morale.

The Psychology Behind Effective Communication in The Workplace

Your brain reacts to any stimuli that it encounters (Chadwick, 2014). When you experience stress, fear, anxiety, happiness, satisfaction and joy, your brain takes those emotions and it processes them through reactions from the limbic system (Moawad, 2017). When our brains experience a negative emotion like stress, this then has a negative knock-on effect on our brains and our emotional wellbeing. Your focus becomes decreased, your ability to concentrate becomes inhibited and your general cognitive abilities are reduced. This can have many side effects in the workplace. If you are not able to focus, you may misunderstand a direction or make a simple mistake that could drastically affect some other areas of the work.

Positive emotions have just the opposite effect on the brain. When you are experiencing positive emotions and positivity in the workplace, you are more likely to be able to focus better and will be able to perform better on tasks that are cognitively demanding, such as creative thinking, cognitive flexibility and faster processing of information.

When an employee is being yelled at or they are becoming overly stressed out about something, this puts them into the flight, fight or freeze mode. You see, your brain can not process whether or not a threat is real or perceived. This is due to the production of cortisol, also known as the stress hormone. When you are experiencing stress, no matter if it is real or perceived, you produce cortisol. So if your boss is screaming at you or you are freaking out over a mistake, your brain processes this the same way as if you were being chased by a tiger. This triggers physiological responses that take energy away from your prefrontal cortex, which helps us to think logically and rationally. So, if your prefrontal cortex is not able to process things correctly, it makes it very difficult to be productive at work.

Why You Need Effective Communication in The Workplace

There are so many reasons to advocate for healthy and positive communication in the workplace. Here are some of the core reasons to promote effective communication at work (Richason, 2017):

- It creates a healthy working environment.
- Helps to remove cultural barriers.
- An increase in bottom-line profits.
- Mitigates conflicts.
- Increases employee engagement.
- Fosters a sense of teamwork.
- Promotes innovation.
- Boosts customer service and satisfaction.
- Increases employee retention.
- Provides transparency within the organization.
- Increased employee productivity.

With all of these benefits, it's no wonder that communication in the workplace is a hot topic.

What Is Internal And External Communication?

There are two basic categories of communication; internal and external (Webb, 2017). Internal communication focuses on the communication between the employee and the company, whereas external communication focuses on the communication outward to customers, clients, vendors or contractors.

Each of these different kinds of communication is handled differently. Internal communications are used to inform, motivate and/or provide feedback to employees. The various forms of internal communications can include internal emails, memos, phone calls, face to face meetings and instant messages. What you say and how you communicate with internal employees is generally different than when you communicate with someone external from the company.

External communications generally take place with customers and other "employees" that are external to the company like vendors or contractors. While external communications can include many of the same types of communications as internal, there are some differences. Your company's website, social media, email newsletter, advertising and so on are all different ways that your company can communicate externally. When your employees communicate via phone, email, text or instant messaging to your customers, this is an external communication.

While each of these types of communications is different, the basic principles behind effective communication can be used for all types, both external and internal.

The Barriers That Prohibit Effective Communication In The Workplace

There is a wide variety of factors that can inhibit effective communication in the workplace; gender, cultural barriers, tone and body language, your brains being hijacked by your emotions, external noise, emotions, and so much more (Zambas, 2019).

First, let's talk about gender. This is a really big one that people might not fully realize is such a barrier to effective communication, particularly in the workplace. Generally speaking, when a woman runs into an issue, she needs to talk it out to help her process the problem and will come to her own solution. This is not her trying to complain but rather work out the problem while talking aloud about it. She is not necessarily seeking a solution to the problem from an external source but rather using what she already has to put together a solution. Men generally think logically and if they need to solve a problem will often seclude themselves while processing the issue at hand. This can create communication barriers in the workplace, just simply because of different genders conversing with each other.

For the most part, men are problem solvers. If a woman comes to them to discuss an issue, he will tend to look for a solution and offer it to them. Generally, if a woman goes to another woman to discuss a problem, she may ask her colleague open-ended questions to help her figure out the solution on her own. If a woman needs to collaborate with a man on something, she should give him explicit instructions as to what needs to be done and what she is expecting.

Men and women also communicate differently with their body language. They can make the same gestures but it will mean two completely different things. A head nod for example. When a woman nods her head she does that as a sign that she is listening; when a man does it, he does it as a sign of agreement (Jenkins, 2018). So you can see how something as simple as a head nod can cause a miscommunication between colleagues.

Cultural barriers can also cause a lack of effective communication in the workplace. Cultural communication barriers can be present when working with colleagues for whom English is their second language and the uses of certain gestures (Gottfried, 2018); such as shaking hands or bowing (Dabbah, 2018). Where one culture might use handshakes to greet one another, another culture will use a bow, which can quickly cause miscommunication. Cultural miscommunications can be internal or external. For example, if a company makes and sells products or services geared toward a specific culture but they do not fully understand it, their message might not come across as intended.

Tone and body language can also be very large barriers to effective workplace communication. The actual words you say in a conversation only account for about 7% of your overall communication. This leaves a lot of room for miscommunication from body language and overall tone. Having your arms crossed while in a conversation with someone shows that you are being closed off, whereas having your arms relaxed at your sides (or talking with your hands) shows that you are open to the conversation and are taking in the information. If you are sitting and speaking with someone, leaning in towards them with your body and feet facing them shows that you are engaged in the conversation. If, on the other hand, you are leaning back in your chair with your body turned or feet facing the door, then this shows that you are not engaged in the conversation and may even signal that you want to get up and leave.

Internal and external noise can also be a very large barrier to effective communication. External noise can include working in a very loud factory; it might be very difficult to effectively speak with someone so they can fully hear and understand everything you are saying to them due to the environmental noises. Internal noise could be trying to listen at a meeting but you are thinking about the argument that you had with your spouse earlier that day instead.

We previously talked about the psychology of effective workplace communication and how your brain plays a role in how well you can communicate with your colleagues. If you are experiencing some kind of internal or external stressor, your physiological responses are going to hijack your brain and cause you to enter the flight, fight or freeze response.

The Importance of A Positive Mindset In The Workplace

The importance of positivity in the workplace cannot be stressed enough. Positivity has been tied to every aspect of success within the workplace such as profit, productivity and satisfaction. Everyone in the workplace can benefit from positivity, both the employer and the employees.

Employers are all about their bottom line and how employees can make them more profitable. Positivity in the workplace increases productivity, thus increasing overall profits. Some of the largest, most profitable companies in the world have figured out that if they keep their employees happy, engaged and positive, their bottom line increases. There is a simple reasoning behind this correlation. Happier employees translate into happier customers. Happier customers tend to buy more and have greater loyalty to the company and become repeat customers and refer friends and family to the company.

A positive environment also leads to a higher retention of a company's good employees. The number one reason that people leave a position or a workplace is that it is in some way negative. It might be a toxic or caustic work environment, somehow negative. It doesn't really matter what they are getting paid; if the work environment is negative, they don't want to work there. Employee retention is highly affected by how positive or negative the work environment is.

There are two aspects of positivity in the workplace; evaluation and creation. If you are a leader or manager of some kind within your workplace, you are likely at some point going to have to evaluate your employees' or team's performance. While it might be easy to see what they could be doing better, this can take a negative overtone. When employees feel that they can never please their employer, that will likely hit their morale. It will only benefit your team if you provide them with a positive evaluation. Let them know that they are doing a good job and you are proud of the work and their commitment to that work. Of course, there are some aspects that they could improve upon, but that is not the focus here. The focus of the evaluation process is to provide your employees with positive feedback. Leave out the *"but!"* Don't go in evaluating your employees like, *"you guys are doing good, but..."* - this is just going to ruin all of the good things that you just said.

While positive evaluation is going to make your team feel great about themselves, you are not staying there. As a manager or leader, give your evaluation, pause and let your employees revel in the positive energy that you have just created, then move on. While your team might be doing well, it is likely that there is some area for improvement that they could be focusing on. When the team focuses on the things they are not excelling at, that creates anxiety. However, when you imagine what you have is going to be better than what you already have, that creates a lot of positive energy and hope within the team. There is a delicate balance between giving a positive evaluation and moving forward to create something even better. When you are communicating with your employees, start with a positive evaluation, move onto the creation of something better and always end on a positive note of encouragement!

How does having a positive work environment benefit the employee? Unless you are completely retired, you are either an employee or self-employed (and might employ other people). If you are an employee, the most obvious benefit of a positive work environment is that you, as the employee, get to be happy. I mean, what is really our most commonly shared goal in life? To be happy! When you look at people's goals, it really doesn't matter what it is, to be their own boss, to make more money, to travel the world, this all leads back to happiness and the experience of happiness. When you are in a work environment that is a positive one, you are going to be happier.

Other benefits to employees of positivity in the workplace are increased job satisfaction, employee retention, productivity, which can also lead to the potential for new opportunities and increases in wage or salary. You might be truly amazed as to how an increase in your own positivity, as an employee, can lead to opportunities both within and outside of the organization. When managers and leaders of an organization continue to see positivity and high levels of production from employees, they want to keep them around and they want to reward them. You might even be presented with opportunities you did not even realize you had available to you.

You see, there is a little secret about positivity that I am going to share with you. It is contagious! When you are positive within one area of your life, it is going to carry over into other areas of your life, such as your love life, your parenting, your finances, and so on.

The Transformative Power of Good Communication In The Workplace

There is a real power to learning how to effectively communicate in the workplace. Effective communication can mitigate conflict, increase employee engagement and create better client relationships while also resulting in a more productive and talented workforce.

Conflict within the workplace results from misunderstandings or feeling misunderstood, not understanding how to communicate with others effectively or when someone feels they are being disrespected or their emotional needs are not being met. When you learn and implement effective communication strategies, misunderstandings can be avoided, you are able to effectively communicate with others and your colleagues will feel respected and that their emotional needs are being met.

Employees become more engaged in the workplace using good communication through connecting with people (Page, 2019). When employees understand what is asked of them, they are able to become aligned with the company's goals and objectives while establishing good communication with their team members. There are several areas in which effective communication can help to improve overall employee engagement. As an employer, it gives you the tools to fully understand the goals and needs of your employees. It gives you the information you need to understand your employees' goals and needs. It provides a better connection and understanding with your employees' skills and talents that you may not have otherwise noticed. It will also give you the ability to cultivate those talents while being cohesive with the company's goals and values. It can improve your connections with coworkers and colleagues to create a more satisfying and positive working environment, as well as build a better relationship with leaders and managers within the organization.

Having effective communication in the workplace also creates a better relationship with clients and customers. Customer and client relationships are at the core of all organizations. Client-facing employees can make or break an organization and be the difference between a satisfied or disgruntled customer. When employees understand how to effectively communicate with customers, it helps them to understand the customer's needs and help the customer to feel understood. It also enables staff to resolve and mitigate any conflicts the customer might have. Effective communication can also help the employee to present information to the customer in a new way that will help the customer to be more receptive.

Furthermore, the workplace will become more productive and increase its talent when it has effective communications strategies in place. When employees are engaged at work they are more productive. When employees are productive and engaged, this helps the leadership team to understand their employees' talents and skills. Employees also become more committed to their workplace and organizations can expect a higher level of buy-in from their employees. Workplaces that focus on effective communication help to foster innovation and creative thought as employees feel safe to express their ideas to their leadership team. This also helps employees to take ownership of their projects and challenges while encouraging creative brainstorming. Leaders will then take notice and use these new found creative brainstorming processes and innovation to build more strategic teams based on employees' strengths.

When applying for jobs, effective communication skills can help to set people apart from other applicants. Ineffective communication in the workplace will ultimately lead to unmotivated employees and employees questioning their ability and confidence within the organization. When there is consistent and effective communication in the workplace, the company is equipped for growth. Growing a company requires both internal and external communication. The company must ensure they are delivering a consistent message externally to their clients and customers.

There are several ways to improve communication within your organization to ensure that employees and the organization are reaching their full potential. You should establish clearlier defined goals and expectations. The leadership team needs to ensure that the goals and expectations for their employees are clear and achievable. They also need to make sure that all of their employees are aware of and understand the objectives of the project as well as the department and organization as a whole. Whatever the message is that is being delivered, it should be clear and your intended audience should easily be able to understand it. When speaking to your intended audience you should always remember to speak politely and plainly so that your message is delivered without offense or confusion.

You must also consider which medium you are choosing to deliver your message through. While, more often than not, face to face communication is preferred, it is not always possible. This can be especially true for virtual teams. When you have to send a message via print or virtually, read it aloud to ensure that it comes across as you are intending it to. In a professional setting, you should avoid the use of emojis or overly expressive text and write in a neutral font and tone.

It is best to keep everyone involved in the process and projects by use of frequent updates and progress reports. This, again, is especially important when working with a remote team. Keeping everyone involved and the lines of communication open will help to ensure that everyone is on the same page while having a less likely chance that miscommunications will occur.

Listening is just as important (if not more important) in the workplace as talking. When you are in a conversation with someone, be engaged with your listening and show empathy. Communicating with someone is a two-way street. The company and the employee will thrive when dialog is encouraged and respect is shown.

While good communication might come easily and even naturally to some, it can be difficult for others to accurately express how they are feeling or the message they are trying to get across. A lack of effective communication can lead to conflict and fundamental errors that could ultimately be avoided if those communicating just understood the message. Just as you can experience miscommunications outside of the workplace, they can happen equally easily within the workplace. It has been shown that 70% of mistakes in businesses are due to a lack of effective communication (Allan, 2019).

Efficiency also increases in the workplace when employees practice good communication. When poor communication happens, efficiency is compromised in addition to the quality of work. On the other hand, when instructions are clear and concise, this eliminates any need to clarify or correct any issues that might arise. If you happen to be an effective communicator but those around you are not so great, make sure you are asking the right questions to get the answers and clarification that you need in order to proceed without confusion.

When there is good communication in the workplace, employee loyalty increases.

Employees feel comfortable discussing issues that might arise and feel free to express their ideas with their leadership team. This helps to build trust and loyalty among team members and the management team. This also eliminates the need for management to micromanage employees and gives them more autonomy within their roles.

Chapter Summary

Technology can greatly inhibit effective communication within the workplace. We send quick emails and memos thinking that our point will get across or our message will be effectively communicated, but this is not always true. Technology alone can not express how we are feeling and lacks non-verbal cues, which can lead to misunderstandings and misinterpretations of the message you were trying to send.

Before you are able to effectively communicate in the workplace, you first need to identify and be able to move past any potential barriers. This can include gender biases, stereotypes and cultural barriers in order to effectively communicate with your colleagues and/or employees. Here are some of the most common barriers to communication in the workplace:

- Gender differences.
- Inattentive listening.
- A miscommunication in body language.
- Not getting the whole story and or jumping to conclusions.
- Inappropriate verbal and non-verbal reactions.
- A negative outlook.

You must understand that when it comes to stress in the workplace or any other area of life, our brains can not perceive whether or not a threat is real or perceived. Therefore your brain is not able to determine if the stress you are experiencing is real or not real.

There are many reasons why you need effective communication in the workplace, such as increasing bottom-line profits and providing transparency within the organization. You can ensure that you are promoting effective communication in the workplace both internally and externally through recognizing and removing gender and cultural barriers, being aware of both verbal and nonverbal communication and minimizing noise.

Positive communication in the workplace is also very important. The more positive the employee, the more productive they are, which then leads to higher profits. Leaders should always ensure that they are providing their workforce with positive feedback.

There is a real power to mastering effective communication in the workplace. It helps to stomp out conflict, increase employee engagement, build and maintain healthier client relationships and results in a happier and more productive workforce.

In the next chapter, you will learn how to develop effective and persuasive communication skills in the workplace.

Chapter Two: How to Develop Effective and Persuasive Communication Skills at Work

Now that we have outlined why you should learn to effectively communicate in the workplace, it is time to outline exactly HOW. This includes everything from verbal and non-verbal communication including body language and being aware of your facial expressions. Now is the time to become a better listener at work and learn how to explain what you are trying to communicate to your colleagues. As a team member in your workplace, you need to learn to become an inclusive communicator and be able to communicate with people from all different backgrounds and all different levels of management.

It is also beneficial to learn persuasive techniques in order to persuade team members and your leadership team to your points of view. These techniques can be used if you have found a better, more efficient way of doing things but others are still stuck in the *"we have always done it this way,"* mentality. Whether you are a leader or member of management in your workplace or are a "low-level" employee, you should be equipped with the skills to both give and receive criticism and be able to share meaningful feedback in a tactful and positive manner.

Your written communications can also have a large effect on how well you communicate with your coworkers. When you speak with someone about an issue or a project, are you asking the right questions to get to the bottom of things or clarify your role? In this chapter, we are going to cover what kinds of questions to ask to get the information that you desire, as well as the secrets to being a proactive communicator, and how to report professionally.

Sending Messages: Verbal and Non-Verbal Communication Skills

There are two main types of communication that humans use; verbal and non-verbal. Each of them sends messages to another party (S. 2019). Verbal communication includes both writing and speaking. It is the words that you say and the words that you write. Non-verbal communication includes everything else and accounts for about 90% of your overall communication. Non-verbal communication includes body language, facial expressions and even sign language (Frost, 2016). The chances of a miscommunication are much greater with non-verbal language than with verbal language.

Verbal communication, which is what you are currently experiencing reading this book, is the most effective form of communication and it can be used to quickly and easily transmit information and or feedback. The communication can be oral, such as a face-to-face conversation, phone calls, lectures, videos and seminars or written, which includes email, text messages, handwritten or typed letters, and so on.

Within the realms of verbal communication, there is also formal and informal. It is likely that most of the communication that you do while at work, will be formal. Formal communication follows a predefined channel in order for the sender to get the information to the receiver. The opposite is true for informal communication: the sender and receiver do not follow any kind of predetermined outline. A work memo would be considered a formal communication, while an example of informal could be a quick text to your coworkers.

Non-verbal communication is something else entirely. There are many, many different types of non-verbal communication. There is chronemics, which is the punctuality and the speed at which the person is speaking. Have you ever met someone who talked really fast about something? What was your impression? Most likely you thought that person was excited about what they were talking about. Although there are many other factors that come into play. Such as the vocalics; this is the volume, tone and pitch of someone's voice. If someone is talking very loudly, they could be upset or just be trying to talk over other environmental noise.

Then we move into the external kinds of non-verbal communication. Haptics is the use of touch when someone is communicating, as a way for them to express their emotions and feelings. This would be something like rubbing someone's arm as you are verbally trying to comfort them. Kinesics is the body language, gestures, posture and facial expressions that a person uses while communicating (more on that soon). The distance at which someone places themselves when communicating to others is known as proxemics. This generally includes different amounts of space for intimate, personal, social and public relationships. People can also communicate non-verbally through their artifacts; this includes the way they dress, their accessories or lifestyle. You are likely to communicate to someone differently (especially with your non-verbal language) if they are wearing a suit than if they are wearing workout clothes.

How To Use and Understand Body Language

Your body language says a lot about who you are and sends a lot of signals to your fellow coworkers. We all do our best to make a good impression on those we work with by carefully choosing our words, but you might not realize how big a stake in your communication that your body language contributes. Without even realizing it, you might be sabotaging your best efforts with your colleagues and clients just by how you are communicating with your body language. You can use body language in the workplace to improve your communication and help to make a positive impression. The use of body language can be intentional or completely unconscious. Your body language has a very strong influence on how other people perceive you. Some examples of poor body language include rolling your eyes, slouching or folding your arms in front of you. When you realize how your body language is received and perceived by others this can help you to communicate more effectively.

A very effective use of body language in the workplace is to maintain eye contact while speaking to someone. When you maintain eye contact while you are speaking to someone or they are speaking to you, this portrays that you are showing interest, paying attention, that you feel confident and are communicating honestly. If you are speaking to someone and you don't maintain eye contact with them, they may feel that you are being dishonest. If someone is speaking to you and you avert your gaze, they may feel that you are not paying attention to them. Posture is also a very useful body language tool. When you slouch or slump in your chair, others will think that you are uninterested in what is going on. When you maintain an erect posture, it shows your attentiveness and engagement in the conversation or communication. If you are sitting and speaking to someone you should lean towards them slightly rather than lean back in your chair. This is another way to show engagement and that you are paying attention to what they are saying.

It is important to be aware of your own body language but also the body language of others around you. When you are speaking with a person or listening to them, be aware of their body language and how they move when they are talking. Other people's body language can help you to determine the kind of message that they are trying to deliver. Are they lacking confidence? If an employee is lacking confidence in a particular area, perhaps they could use additional training or support to help them thrive. If you sense that they are lacking in certain areas, try to nicely call them out on it without making them feel uncomfortable. Saying something as simple as, *"Hey [name], do you recall when we spoke about [topic], I got the sense that you are lacking confidence in [task], how can I help you become more confident in that area?"* Saying it this way lets your colleague know that you are not trying to be rude but to help them reach their full potential.

You can also use the skill of reading people's body language when you are giving a presentation or lecture. Being able to effectively gauge the body language of your audience will help you to determine how your message is being received. You should easily be able to tell how engaged your audience is by their eye contact, posture and other body movements. If your audience is lacking eye contact, tend to be fidgeting a lot with pens or phones and are slouching and leaning back in their chairs, they are probably disengaged with the message you are trying to send.

If an employee disagrees with the speakers' message, they will use their body language to signal that as well. When people feel threatened or unsafe in some way - this can even just be a simple disagreement in a message they are receiving - they will become closed off. Their body language might include turning their feet or whole body away from you, crossing their arms or leaning back in their chairs. Pay close attention, if you see this happening, try and open up the discussion to see if you can figure out what your audience disagrees with you on. Ask them for solutions to the issues.

While, with a little practice, you can understand your colleagues' body language and should be able to recognize how they are feeling, misinterpreting body language can have a drastically different effect. When body language is misinterpreted, that can lead to friction, conflict and misunderstandings of all kinds. The likelihood of communication misunderstandings only increases as a workplace becomes more diverse and cultural differences might come into play. If you are communicating with someone in your workplace and they seem to be showing negative body language, that could mean they are frustrated, bored or being dishonest. You should respond before you react. Reacting to body language will only lead to further friction and conflict. Do your best to investigate their body language and feelings further. Ask your colleague additional questions that could shed some light on their body language and how they are feeling. There is an upside to all of this though, the longer you work with someone, the more you get to know their body language and be able to read their body language becomes easier over time.

Here are some of the body language mistakes that you are making at work that you might not even realize:

- Having bad posture or slouching.
- Fidgeting.
- Having a tense expression on your face.
- Being too casual.
- Not making eye contact or looking down.
- Crossing your arms.
- Standing too close to people.

It takes some time to become aware of your body language, how your body language affects other people and to be able to understand other's body language. Just as with any other skill, the more you practice it the better you will become at it. So when you are in conversation with someone, pay attention to how they are using their body and how they are responding to your body language.

How to Become Aware of Your Facial Expressions

Your facial expressions also play into your body language and how people perceive you. Your facial expression is your first impression when meeting others; this includes customers, colleagues and clients. The expressions that you make with your face are inherently used for social cues and to give others around you clues as to how you are feeling. Your facial expression can affect the trajectory of the conversation or social interaction (Russell, 2015). Even if you don't mean to, your facial expressions can give away your feelings and this can lead to people perceiving you in a certain light in the workplace. Here are three situations that you might find yourself in where your facial expressions are giving away more than you want them to.

When you greet someone at work that you do not like. When you don't like someone and are in their presence, you may often express this through a scowl on your face. This can be detrimental to your working relationships as it shows that person and others around you that you do not like that individual. When you are greeting someone that you don't like, trying to greet them with a slight smile will always leave a better impression than a scowl or frown.

Unforeseen circumstances in your workload can also show on your facial expressions. This can happen when you get an increase in your workload; your facial expression might indicate that you feel that you can not handle it, with a furrowed brow or pout on your face. Ensure that your facial expressions don't indicate to your other colleagues that you feel you are incapable of the hard work you are being asked to do.

Generally, you smile when you are happy, and often when you receive a compliment, however, this facial expression comes off differently when you are in the workplace. A smile when you receive a compliment can make you come across as smug, and you don't want this! When you receive a compliment on something you did well on, just say *"thank you,"* give a polite nod and give a slight smile to acknowledge the positive comment you received. You don't want to seem like you have a big ego when you give a big smile showing all of your teeth; gloating doesn't go over very well in the workplace.

That's not to say that you should try and avoid showing facial expressions at work, it simply means that you should be aware of the facial expression that you are showing and how they can be perceived by those around you.

The Keys to Becoming a Better Listener at Work

Being a good listener at work can be difficult sometimes, especially if there is a lot of environmental noise. There are a few key things that you can do to practice better listening skills at work. The easiest is being quiet and letting the other person speak without trying to think of what you are going to say to them right away. Secondly, if you are engaging in a two-way conversation, repeat back to that person what you heard them say. *"So what I am hearing you say is [this], did I get that correct?"* Not only does this validate to the sender of the message that you are paying attention and actually listening to them, it also helps to eliminate any misunderstandings.

Many people are not very good listeners. All too often people might hear what someone is saying but they are not truly listening; if you are a parent, you know this well. People also listen to see when they can start talking. You can learn a lot from a person just by listening to them and letting them talk. Keep this in mind; we have one mouth and two ears, therefore we should listen twice as much as we talk.

Becoming a better listener can help you to deepen your relationship to the person you are communicating with (Edberg, 2019). This works both in the workplace and in your personal life. People often have a difficult time listening because they feel that they don't personally gain anything from it. When you truly listen to someone, it is likely that they will listen better to you as well. The main point of listening is to understand what the person is trying to communicate to you.

Listening to someone speak is like playing a game of memory. When you are trying to remember what someone is saying, try and process the information like you have to tell someone else about it later. Even if you don't actually have to repeat the information, this can be very helpful in recalling information from the conversation. This will help you to be more alert and even ask more questions to help you understand what the person is trying to communicate to you. This should also help you to focus more on what the person is saying and to stop thinking so much about what you are going to say next.

Did you know your eyes can help you to become a better listener? Maintaining eye contact during a conversation can help you to focus on what the other person is saying, thus helping you to retain more information. If you have issues or feel weird about staring someone in the eyes, look directly at the center of their nose, they will never know the difference.

Cut out technological distractions. This is a BIG one! It is very difficult to be able to effectively listen to someone when you are scrolling through your phone or on your computer. This can lead to misunderstanding what the other person is saying or completely missing points of the conversation. When you are on your phone or computer it also makes the other person feel as though you are not listening to them.

You can let the other person know you are listening by summarizing what they said. When you are able to summarize what was said this lets them know that you were listening and that you have understood what was said. This also helps to clear up any potential misunderstandings that might otherwise occur.

While it would be great if you could read people's minds to mitigate any misunderstandings, you cannot. You can, however, ask questions to clarify what is being said. Try and stick to open-ended questions to gain a further understanding of what they are trying to communicate to you. Asking open-ended questions also encourages them to open up and explore what they are saying and dive more in-depth into the conversation.

You can also be a better listener when you are prepared to listen. If you know that you are going into a long meeting that could potentially put you to sleep, make sure you are mentally and physically prepared to listen. It is difficult enough to listen, much less understand the message someone is trying to get across when you are falling asleep or feeling foggy. In order to get your mind working and prepared for an intake of information, get some fresh air! You can do this by opening a window in your office (if you have any) or going for a short walk outside. You can also just do a bit of exercise to get your blood flowing to your brain.

When you listen, you just need to listen. Don't think about adding your input, interrupting the sender or jumping to solutions or conclusions. Just try and be present in the moment and fully listen to understand what the sender is saying. Sometimes when people are talking, all they really need is someone to listen to them so that they can vent or work out their own issues.

If for whatever reason you are not able to give someone your full attention and listen to them, be honest about it. Let them know that you are too tired, busy or distracted at this point to hold a valuable conversation and ask them if it is possible to continue it later. Set a time that you feel that you will both be able to have a conversation with minimal noise interference.

How to Become a Better Communicator at Work Through Better Explanation

You can't make everyone be a more effective communicator. You can do your best, however, to make sure you are explaining things to the best of your ability. We talked quite a bit earlier about how your body language has a very large effect on how your colleagues perceive you at work. Body language is one area you can focus on to help you better explain the message you are trying to get across. Make sure that the words that you are saying and the message that your body language and your tone of voice are giving off are all cohesive. Saying that you are excited to start on a new project while having a somber tone and a frown sends conflicting messages.

Asking questions in a conversation goes both ways. When you are speaking with someone or an audience, ask them periodically if they understand or if something needs more explanation. Checking in with people to ensure that they are understanding what you are communicating will also help you to sharpen your explanation skills.

Diversified Work Environments: How to Become a More Inclusive Communicator

First of all, I would like to address what inclusive communication actually is. It's unfortunate that this still happens, but discrimination in the workplace is still very prevalent today, particularly between men and women. While women make up about 50% of the workforce, there are less than 15% that hold executive positions (Warner, 2019). While you should already be aware that men and women communicate differently, the discrimination that occurs is often unconscious as it is inadvertently reinforced in everyday conversations. Inclusive communication is a communication style that transcends gender and cultural biases so that each party understands and is understood.

Generally speaking, women are better at bringing a sense of personal connection to the workplace. Workplaces can all too often be stoggy and mechanical. People are going to perform their tasks better when they feel appreciated and heard by their leadership team. Leaders within the organization, whether male or female, should not be afraid of vulnerability, attention or authenticity.

The modern definition of gender is drastically different than the archaic one that most people understand. As employees or employers, we all need to move past that antiquated vision of what gender binary is and include a broader range of identities and genders within the workplace. We can work to overcome gender gaps and unconscious biases through acknowledgment and admission of how these biases have influenced our behaviors, thoughts and feelings.

You must also adjust your speaking and listening styles to be less definitive. While people might be able to easily express facts and ideas, it might be more difficult for them to express their feelings or values. When in conversation, acknowledge the fact or idea and listen for the feelings and values behind it. Paraphrase what your colleague said to you and seek to understand the true meaning behind it.

Along with being able to recognize your own gender biases, you should also be able to recognize and allow for different styles of communication. This is especially crucial for leaders within the organization, regardless of their gender identification. Leaders should work towards maintaining a style of communication that is open and allows for unique perspectives.

In order to become an inclusive and effective communicator, you need to be able to stop talking and genuinely engage with the people you are communicating with. Generally speaking, at work, men speak freely and do not wait for an invitation to talk, whereas women generally wait for a request of their input. Male leaders could then benefit from pausing before talking and making an attempt to reach out to their female counterparts asking for their input, opinions and ideas. This will result in a more productive and diverse work environment. Furthermore, male leaders need to work towards building strong relationships with every member of their team.

As an employee or a leader, you must move past any preconceived notions and stereotypical responses that you carry internally and work to remove your limiting beliefs. Do your best to be open to the person you are having a conversation with, both internally and externally. Focus on building relationships and understanding each other's needs and building trust within your team.

How to Get People to Agree With You: Putting Together an Effective and Persuasive Message

Every day in your workplace you put together messages, in one form or another. Sometimes these messages are meant to convey important information while other times these messages are meant to sway your colleagues in one direction or another on a decision or a topic. You might need to use persuasion in the workplace to get your employees to do something for you, or for your boss to do something for you or even for your colleagues to help you do something. Either way, having an understanding of how to persuade them can be a very beneficial skill to hone. There are numerous things that you can do to help persuade someone in an argument or to assist you with something.

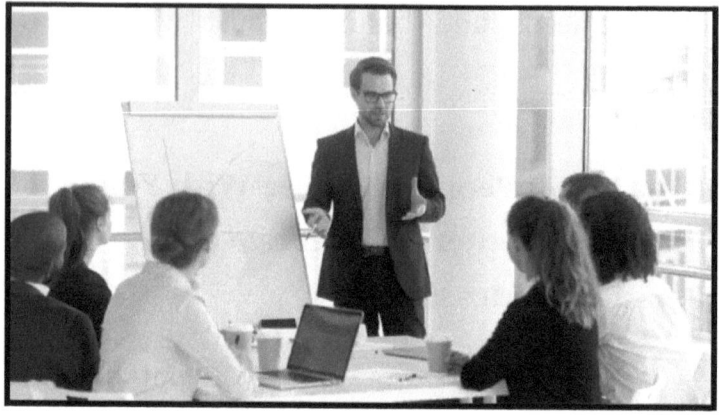

Persuasion is all about influence. The more influence you have over someone or a group of people, the more power you hold to persuade them. There are many common techniques that help to influence people either on purpose or inadvertently, here are six of the most common (Dean, 2010):

- Likability
- Social proof
- Consistency
- Scarcity

- Authority
- Reciprocity

Likability is just that - the more someone likes you the more influence you hold over them. Influencers can successfully create higher likability by using flattery and highlighting similarities with those they are influencing to create and increase attraction. Social proof is like an avalanche effect - the more followers someone has, the more people follow them. You can hold more influence over someone if you do what you say you are going to do and remain consistent in your words and actions. Scarcity has a lot to do with consumerism and creating a fear of missing out on something, but this can also be applied in the workplace to persuade and influence colleagues. Perhaps if your colleagues view your time as being scarce, they will cherish more.

Authority is a major influencer and is often used to persuade people. People are also influenced by experts. When experts flaunt their knowledge, people become aware and are influenced by those experts. Reciprocity is an influence technique that can be easily misused and abused. When someone owes you something they are more likely to be influenced and persuaded by you. However, you should not go around making people indebted to you for your own personal gain.

The persuasiveness of your argument is not just dependent upon you, it is also dependent upon your audience (Dean, 2019). Your argument or point will be more persuasive if it is personally relevant to your audience. If your audience does not find the message relevant, they are going to stop listening to you and no matter what you say you are not going to be persuasive.

When persuading someone you often need to engage in multiple strong arguments in order to get your message across. Generally speaking, the more strong arguments you have with them the more persuasive you will become. While trying to persuade someone on a topic, it is more beneficial to keep your arguments balanced rather than one-sided. Present a two-sided argument but be sure to shut down the counter-argument to ensure your side of the argument is more appealing.

There are three main goals that you should aim for when trying to persuade someone; affiliation, accuracy and positive self-concept. As humans we are social beings, and as such, we all want to be liked by our peers. Likability and reciprocity are both part of the goal of affiliation. When someone is received as likable and reciprocates, it sends the world a message about their sociability. It is in our nature to join and follow influencers which satisfies the goal of affiliation.

Accuracy is all about doing things right. Those that don't care about how to do things properly don't get very far in life or work. People always want to seek for the right answer, which is where the influencer comes into play. Influencers understand our need to be right and are able to offer their expertise or authority which satisfies our need for accuracy. The goal of accuracy ties into the techniques of social proof and scarcity as experts and influencers are more likely to be right and we don't want to miss out on anything.

The last goal of persuasion is a positive self-concept. People have all sorts of self-protective mechanisms. It takes a very long time for individuals to figure out their place in the world and they don't want to lose that. When we have a certain world view, we do whatever we can to keep that view intact. We want to believe that the things we believe in are, in our eyes, good in some way and help to uphold our self-esteem. This is where influencers can slowly start to persuade you. It starts with a small request and then builds up to larger and larger requests. It can be really amazing the lengths that some will go to maintain that positive view of themselves.

When you are trying to persuade people you

should ensure that your message matches your medium. Is what you are trying to persuade people of better received in written or spoken format? Should you speak with them face to face or should you make a video? A very important point is to avoid telling them that you are going to try and persuade them. Doing this will only prime your audience to start preparing their counter arguments when they should be listening to you.

In order to be persuasive, you must first be familiar with your audience. If they are already somewhat in agreement with you then talking slowly is fine. However, if they are not already in agreement with you, then fast talkers can be more persuasive. Repetition is also beneficial in persuading someone to your point of view. Repeating a statement gives it the illusion of truth which can then lead to the reality of persuasion.

Furthermore, you have to also make sure your audience is ready when you are trying to persuade them. This includes having their attention and minimalizing distractions whenever possible. If your audience is distracted or not paying attention they may not think about your message or argument, which makes it very difficult to persuade someone. It has actually been shown that when people are consuming caffeine, they are more easily persuaded as they are more alert. If you are trying to persuade your audience with a very strong message then it is better to have your audience very focused in on what you are saying. If your message is rather weak, then it is actually better to have your audience slightly distracted. If you are a parent, you have probably experienced this. Your child asks you for something when you are in the middle of something else and, without actually thinking about it, you say yes to their request.

In addition, you have to think very carefully on how you frame your messaging so that it is received in the way you want it to be received. Messages with a positive framing are going to be more persuasive. You must also be a little sneaky and disguise your message so as to not have it come across as persuasive. Your message will be more persuasive if it does not seem to be intended as such.

Confidence also plays a huge role in how your argument is perceived, both your confidence and your audience's. When you are confident it will help your audience to feel more confident - as such they should be confident in changing their attitude. Confidence also increases when the argument is coming from a credible source. With confidence comes power. The power the audience will feel to change and the power that the influencer holds over the audience.

Lastly, you should avoid trying to persuade strong beliefs or opinions. These are very difficult to change and often people do not budge on them unless they feel an intrinsic need to do so. Never dive into a persuasive argument when there are long standing beliefs and ideas that your audience is committed to. You will only be met with resistance and objection.

How to Effectively Give and Receive Positive Criticism

For most people, being criticized can really hit their ego and self-esteem. However, if done correctly, criticism and critiquing can inspire and uplift individuals and push them to do better in the workplace. Whether or not you are a leader within your organization, you are likely to have to critique a team member or employee at some point. For many people, giving criticism is difficult. However, receiving critique can be even more difficult. Individuals like to feel like they are doing things correctly and that they are accomplished. It doesn't really matter how nicely you put it, it often hurts to hear the truth about your work performance. If you are someone who is consistently striving to improve your work performance, then you might welcome and value the feedback, even if it hurts. If the giver of the feedback is being neutral or coming from a place of positive feedback rather than trying to make the receiver feel bad, that can actually help to build trust through constructive criticism and empathy.

Whether you are giving criticism to a colleague or a subordinate there are certain measures that you can take in order to make sure that your feedback is well received and appreciated. As the receiver of the feedback there are also actions that you can take in order to fully benefit from your feedback. Now, a word of caution, some feedback you receive you might have a warning for, like an employee review. However, some feedback might be unwanted and you will be caught off guard. In either situation, you can take that feedback and make it advantageous to you.

Make sure that you have clear objections. What is the best possible outcome of the critique? If you are the giver of the feedback, do not simply vent without intention; you are not going to achieve anything other than making the other person resent you. If you are the receiver of such criticism and feel that you have come under attack, then do your best to diffuse any tense situation. You can do this by asking the person who is criticizing you what they hope to accomplish with this interaction. In the best case scenario, you will figure out what the root cause of the friction and criticism is, in the worst case scenario, you can make a graceful exit.

When you are going to critique someone or give them feedback of some sort, first consider the environment and the timing. Pick a neutral environment that is free of distractions. There are many situations in the workplace where criticism takes place in front of other employees which can cause embarrassment and shame to the person receiving the criticism. In some work environments a third party is required if an employee is to be "reprimanded," but this can make people feel like they are being ganged up on, so make sure that the third party is neutral and won't cause further friction. Friction can also be minimized by the use of appropriate humor and rapport that has already been built between parties. You can also help to take down defenses of the person you are giving feedback to by sharing your own silly mistakes and personal experiences. This helps for that person to be able to relate to you before addressing their own performance issues.

If you are the person who is being given the feedback and you are feeling threatened or embarrassed, then don't be afraid to speak up about it. Ask the person who is providing you with the feedback to move to a more private area or if you can set up a meeting at another date and time in the near future. Make sure that you are keeping your body language neutral and being open rather than closed off - this will help the person critiquing you to feel more comfortable and relaxed.

Upon critiquing someone it is wise to use fewer

words with more meaning behind them. It is likely that the person you are critiquing is going to have a strong internal voice that is causing them anxiety. You are likely to be able to get your point across more if you are short and to the point. The more you try and talk to the person that you are critiquing, the less they are likely to hear. They will become distracted from the key points and it will make it more difficult for them to remember the points you are trying to make. Do your best to plan your conversation in advance and if possible write it down so that the person you are communicating with has something to walk away with and remember the conversation by.

If you are on the receiving end of the criticism, it is best to let your critics speak their mind and get everything off of their chest. If you try and debate your position you will come off as defensive and closed off. It is better for you to just take the feedback in that moment and agree while revisiting it later for careful consideration. The person that was critiquing you will take you more seriously when your response is contemplated, well thought out and articulated than if you just react to the situation.

You must not approach a critique in a self-serving manner but be able to know your subject well enough to be able to explain how your feedback will benefit them and help them to achieve their desired goals. The person you are giving the feedback to is going to be more open to suggestions if they are invested in the outcome of the critique. If you are able to provide a context for the critique, such as a promotion, then it then becomes vital to their success.

In contrast, if you are the one that is experiencing the critique, then take an objective look at the situation. Step outside of yourself and the situation and objectively look at what is being said. Are you clear on your goals? Is this critique going to help you further your career or is just someone having a bad day rambling on and using you as a target?

Lastly, learn how to use self-critique. Self-critique is two-sided; learning how to do it for yourself and learning how to encourage others to do it. If you are the person giving the feedback, don't just lay out a list of things that they did wrong, give examples of scenarios using an objective viewpoint and ask your subject questions that encourage them to draw their own conclusions. These self-drawn conclusions should focus on the subject's areas of improvement. Ask them questions that help them to take on a manager's perspective of their situation. Use "I" statements or examples from your own experiences that help to take the focus off of them and puts the focus on how you feel.

When it comes to self-critiquing, you should be doing this on a regular basis. Do your best to try and estimate the key points of any feedback before it actually happens. There is a very effective way to disarm your critiques before they start to criticize you and that is to be able to start a conversation about your own failures before someone else is able to. Not only will this disarm your critics but also impress them. This can turn a potential attack into a win-win for both parties.

The Importance of Clear Written Communication Skills in the Workplace

While many employers stress that employees have effective oral and written communication skills, ensuring effective written communication can often be overlooked. When an employee has very effective written communication skills, it can benefit the company in multiple ways, such as ensuring quality communication with customers. Employees with good written communication skills are viewed as intelligent, courteous and detail-oriented.

There is the old adage that you only get one chance to make a first impression, this holds true for written communications as well. The reader of the written communication will form a good impression of the writer if the writing is well-written, organized and free of grammatical errors. Good written communication during the job application process can be crucial to a job offer and increased salary. If an employee has poor writing skills in an external communication, this can reflect poorly on the company overall. If an employee has poor writing skills and their colleagues notice a pattern of poor writing skills, they will likely be viewed as unintelligent (Petersen, 2019).

Excellent written communication skills demonstrate courtesy on the part of the writer. When someone takes the time with their written communications, this shows that they value the reader's time. The reader also benefits from the writer presenting their ideas in a clear and organized manner. If the writer is not able to clearly communicate their message, this takes time and energy from the reader to try and determine what the message is that is trying to be delivered. The reader might even have to ask clarifying questions to try and figure out what the writer is trying to communicate.

Clear communication is vital to sound business decisions both internally and externally. It is much easier for employees to understand projects and to share ideas when objectives are clearly defined and easily understood. For external communications, employees, customers and vendors can more easily understand one another when written communications are clear and free of potential misunderstandings. It is much easier to coordinate goals, meetings and negotiations when written communications are straightforward.

If you are not inherently good at written communications, you can hone your skills here too. There are several ways in which you can work to improve your written communication skills.

Take your time when writing. So often, people make simple and silly mistakes in their writing when they rush. Take your time writing then go back and proofread what you have written. Do not rush through your written communications as quickly as possible but rather as individual mini projects. Always use a grammar checker when writing. Make sure your computer is equipped with a grammar checker or install one. Don't be afraid to ask for feedback from your colleagues. If you are writing an especially important email, be sure to have your manager or coworker read through the email before sending it on to its recipient. If you feel that you really need some extra help with your writing, take a course on written communications. Most community colleges offer written communications classes and there are also many available online.

The Secret to Being a Proactive Employee at Work

To be proactive means to act before a future event happens; you are causing things to happen rather than just waiting and reacting to things when and as they happen (Scivicque, 2018). Proactive employees are resourceful and are not passive. When employees are proactive they don't need to be micromanaged, they require less detailed instructions from their leadership team and often don't need to be asked to do things and can anticipate the needs of their team. Being proactive can apply to the individual role of the employee or to any extra roles and responsibilities of their team and/or organization. When employees are proactive within their own roles they may find a more effective and productive way of completing their own responsibilities. When an employee is proactive in roles that are outside of their defined job description, this speaks to their organizational citizenship behaviors. An employee with a high organizational citizenship behavior and who is proactive will be more likely to ask their colleagues or manager if they need assistance on a project before being asked to help (Cooley, 2019).

Proactive employees think and act in certain ways that help them to move themselves and their organizations forward.

Employees who are proactive are organized. Their workspace is organized, their schedule is organized and they maintain a positive mindset. When employees are organized and are able to effectively manage their time, they approach tasks in a more effective manner which also allows them to be open to more possibilities in the workplace. A positive mindset in the workplace encourages the employee and their colleagues to look for the best in all situations. Employees who are organized, take stock of situations and remain positive are looked at as ready, willing and able to take on greater responsibilities. They are often viewed as the go-to person and a key problem solver on the team or in the organization. In order to become a more proactive employee, take stock of your current roles and responsibilities within the organization and ask yourself these questions:

- What are your priorities and tasks?
- Which of your priorities can be eliminated, consolidated or shortened?
- What are your regular or less urgent tasks and how can you stay ahead of them?
- When problems arise, how do you solve them?
- How can you plan ahead or anticipate problems before they develop?
- How could you automate tasks to make your work less time consuming and to be more efficient?
- Are there any tasks that you could delegate or that would be better suited for other employees?

Asking yourself these questions and answering them can help you to increase your productivity and become a more proactive employee or leader.

Look around at your coworkers and leaders - is there someone you admire? Someone who always seems to be ahead of the game and everyone seems to go to when an issue arises? If you can, try to spend time with that person and observe their behaviors and gain insight from them. Use what you can learn from them and adapt your own techniques. Some of their techniques might work better for you than others. You need to work to build up your own repertoire and fine-tune the things that work for you and get rid of what doesn't. Let your management or leadership team know that you want to help more or take on greater responsibilities. Don't sit around and wait for someone to ask you to help. You need to be ready and willing to make your own opportunities and show that you want to be more involved and take on more responsibilities.

Goal setting is a very large part of being proactive. Write down your goals and set deadlines! A goal without a deadline is simply a dream. When you know what you want, it is easier to work towards your outcomes. Small goals can lead to larger goals, so think about working backward. If your goal is to be promoted, then be proactive and figure out how to work backward. This could mean showing your leadership skills by taking on more difficult tasks or working with other employees to help solve problems. Don't get discouraged by setbacks or obstacles that you run into. You have to be willing to step outside of your comfort zone and be resilient when overcoming obstacles. You should be committed to always doing your best work and work on being a role model to others on your team and within your organization. Show that you are passionate about what you are doing and give it your all, even if it's a project that you don't particularly want to work on. Managers and other leaders will take notice.

Being proactive takes a lot of work, so celebrate your successes, no matter how big or small. You have to remain flexible, you can't anticipate every outcome. You need to be able to respond rather than react to unexpected situations; this is a good quality of a proactive employee. While there are certainly situations where it is appropriate to react, proactive employees are flexible and able to manage many different situations.

How to Ask The Right Questions That Get Results

Our brains are wired to ask questions, but in order to get answers that get results, you need to be asking the right questions (Grace, 2018). Asking questions is as much an art as it is a science. If your role in your organization is to get results and keep things moving forward, then you should be well versed in asking questions - quality questions, that is. The quality of the questions that you ask determine the quality of the answers you will receive. Generally speaking, when you start a question with "why," it is unlikely that you will get the answer you are looking for or that any new information will be revealed.

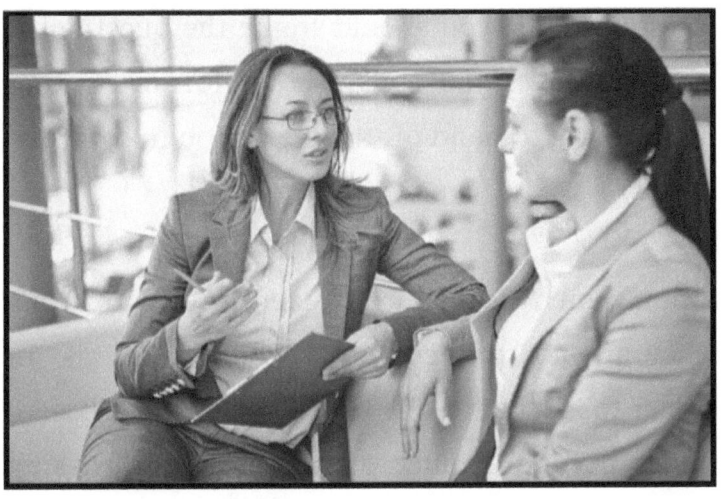

When you start a question with "why," it sounds as though you are placing blame on the person you are speaking with. "Why," questions do not open up dialog and conversation that will lead to getting to the heart of the issue but are often used to confirm a suspicion. When trying to find an answer, asking the right question is half of the battle. Asking "why" questions also puts the person you are asking the question to, in a position that will lead the answer to sound defensive. When you ask "why" questions, you are being lazy as it puts all of the thinking onto the receiver of the question. In order to effectively ask questions, you should frame the question so that it moves the conversation forward rather than trying to hand off the resolution to someone else.

Management teams are trained to give answers, they are not trained to ask good questions. In order to ask better questions, you should observe more beyond a quick glance. Instead of asking why your team didn't finish a project on time, you could ask questions like:

- Which of my team members seem distracted and which seem to be on track?
- Are there any skill sets that the team is missing?
- When does my team seem to produce

their best work?
- How do the team dynamics affect the project outcomes?

You see the different areas of concern that are being addressed rather than just placing blame on the team that the project wasn't finished on time. There are many different aspects that could lead to a team not completing the project on time. Perhaps some team members are putting in the work they need to while others are slacking. Or perhaps there are some external factors that are affecting the team's outcomes. Being able to observe your team will help you to ask quality questions that spark further conversation and get to the root cause of issues.

People who are curious tend to be in a better position to be asking the right questions. When professionals like engineers get curious about something, they go deep into the topic. Don't just look for what is obvious or what is on the surface of the issue. Leave all of your judgments and preconceived notions at the door. When you are curious about something, this also opens you up to vulnerability as you can admit that you don't have all of the answers. When it comes to professional and scientific studies, researchers don't hide their mistakes, they publish them in order to help advance their fields. Instead of asking why you (or your team) is failing to find answers you should explore your curiosity. Take a different approach to asking questions curiously. Focus on questions like this:

- What does the solution to this problem look like?
- How would the end-user see this issue and solution?

Try and look at the problem from all different angles and come up with various perspectives. Ask other people their perspective on the issue or check to see what others have done in similar situations, which leads me to my next point, recognizing patterns.

When you are able to recognize patterns in problems you can then arrive at a solution quicker. When you are able to get the pattern right you can then scale your design as it should consistently work. Instead of focusing on why you have not yet found a solution, focus on what has already worked and how you can consider the problem from a different perspective.

Quality questions also show empathy. Genuine and quality questions are not leading in nature nor do they ask for anything in return. The questions you are asking should not be about trying to find the quickest or easiest solution but rather finding a long-term solution. Get to the root of the problem and stop asking why the problem exists but rather how you can get closer to the source of the issue. Here are some empathetic questions to consider:

- How can your team get closer to the source of the issue?
- What can each individual do to help

realize the issue at hand?
- What can you do to make the solution more practical and easier to understand?

Finally, you must be present and engaged when asking questions. Being present is about understanding the culture surrounding the issue and being able to change the lens in which you view the problem. Changing the lens can mean looking to different environments and industries to observe how others might be resolving issues. Instead of asking why a product or service is not selling you need to look beyond the product or service itself and look to the consumers. Ask instead:

- Are the buyers experiencing resistance of some kind?
- What can you do to remove barriers to the customers?

Asking truly effective questions stems from

incorporating all five of the aforementioned areas. You must be able to observe, bring curiosity to the problem, be able to recognize patterns surrounding the issue, empathize with the end user and be present in cultural differences. Quality question asking provides a sense of ownership that promotes leveraged thinking by revealing concepts. You can start to ask better questions by utilizing creative thinking, openness and inclusivity.

How to Professionally Report to Your Leadership Team on a Project Status

Developing a professional report on a project that you are working on can go a long way to showcasing your communication skills to your leadership team. Being able to professionally report on the status of a project is not something that many people are skilled at; even the best project managers can struggle with this. It simply comes down to a lack of understanding from the perspective of the project manager (Redmond,

2018). Your manager is most likely being pressed for information from their manager on the status of the project and it has now ended up in your lap on the reporting of the project status. There are a few basic rules that you can adhere to, to build your reputation as someone who knows how to effectively report on the status of a large and important project. You will be able to keep your management team informed and keep the project successfully moving forward.

First and foremost, you need to take on the perspective of your manager or management team which you will be reporting to. If you are the one in charge of reporting the status of an important project then it shouldn't come as a surprise that your manager is going to consume any important information on the project that they can get. If you are able to build an excellent report on the status of the project, your manager doesn't have to worry about getting involved and can remain informed about the health and direction of the project. Your boss needs to regularly obtain information about the project in order to share with their boss. When you are on top of things, your boss will also look like they are on top of things which can be a benefit to you.

Even if you are working on a project that is less important, you should take the reporting of that project just as seriously. It is beneficial to your manager to be able to look at a short report for a project that they can easily skim over the details of to ensure that everything is on track. Your job in being able to professionally report a project comes down to being able to distil all of the information into easily digestible chunks that are simple to understand while presenting the most basic and essential elements of the project. There are three main components to writing an excellent project status report. You must include the three main components (overall, milestones and issues), how to organize the status of your report, what brief details to include, the key data to include, any issue management and the expected results.

The three main components that you should be including in your project report that will have your manager jumping for joy over your stellar project reporting skills are the overall, milestones and issues. The overall of the project is the general overall health of the project. The management team should be able to detect if the project is in trouble. As the one reporting on the project, you might not be aware of all the issues of the project and your manager should be able to quickly determine if the project is in trouble from what you are reporting. The next important component is the project milestones. The milestones are major accomplishments that have been completed at specific dates. Managers should be able to see which milestones have been completed, which ones are on track and which might be behind. This allows the management team to see an overall view of the schedule of the project and help them to adjust accordingly if necessary. Lastly, the third major component of the project that you should report on, is any issues that have arisen. If there have been any obstacles for the successful completion of the project, you should be sure to include these in your report. This helps the management team determine if they need to make adjustments or step in and offer further assistance.

Up next is being able to effectively organize your project report. You should be starting at the highest level and working your way down to the lower level stuff. Make sure to put the overall project health first; this way, a manager can immediately tell if something needs to be done with the project. If the manager is concerned about the overall project health they can look at further details within the project health, look at scheduled dates and the issues that could be affecting the project deadlines. If you are really good at reporting, you should be able to report the issues that are causing the most issues by priority.

In addition, your project report should include the brief details. They need to be clear, concise and crisp in order for the management team to quickly consume them with little effort. Considering your manager likely has many projects that they are managing, they have very little time to sit down and read your project report, so make sure you are only including the details that they absolutely need to know. You don't need to narrate your project report but rather be as to the point as possible. For example, rather than writing in paragraphs, use short, bulleted points. Reduce the information as much as possible without cutting out any vital information. Avoid adding any adverbs and adjectives or any unnecessary labeling. For example, do not put "date: 1/2/2019" but rather just the date as "1/2/2019" already signifies a date and does not need explanation.

You must ensure that all key data is included in your project report. This will let your management team know the overall health of the project, the project milestones and any issues that are present. The key data points that you should be including in your project report are:

- The name of the project.
- Any project identification numbers or other identifiers.
- The overall health of the project.
- The percentage you expect to be completed at certain milestones.
- The percentage that are actually completed at certain milestones.
- The number of days you are ahead or behind on the project.
- The number of issues that you are facing preventing the project from moving forward.
- The number of any "normal" issues the project is experiencing.

These elements of data should provide a sound enough overview of the project that your leadership can take a quick look over. Your leadership team needs to see more than just the overall health of the project, they need to be able to see a very quick overview of the timeline, milestones and issues to determine if they should get involved and assist the project. When giving an overview on project milestones you should include the milestone name, the percentage of completion of the milestone, the planned start and finish date and the actual start and finish date. There are many different ways to present the milestones using colors and fancy charts. Don't go for what looks best, go for what is the most practical and easy to understand. You want to create clarity, not more confusion.

When it comes to communicating project issues, you should present these at the end of your project report. This section should include all the various things your leadership team needs to know about the issues the project is experiencing. This can include the ticket number if you have some kind of project issue ticketing system, the name of the issue, the date and time the issue was reported, the priority or severity of the issue, the name of the person who is currently handling the issue, the estimated time the issue is going to be resolved and the current activity of the issue.

Once you have become great at communicating with your leadership team on the status of projects, one of two things will generally happen. Either your leadership team will talk to you less because they feel that you have everything under control, or they will converse with you more to try and stay on top of any issues and get more details out of you. They are less likely going to be constantly asking you about the status of the project as you will already have provided it to them. If your management team is still asking you for status reports, you are either not sending them enough, not sending them to the right people or not sending a good enough status report. Your leadership team should not have to continuously ask you for status reports but rather be able to passively consume them. Employees that are able to produce quality project reports are few and far between. An employee that can present a project in a clear and concise manner is much more beneficial to the company than someone who can make fancy charts and graphs.

Chapter Summary

Developing effective communication skills at work is something that anyone is capable of. With your communication toolbox stocked full, you can persuade management, get your employees on board and ensure that your message is always being effectively communicated.

There are many ways to communicate both verbally and non-verbally. Considering that 90% of your overall communication is non-verbal, it is very important that you are well aware of your body language and other non-verbal cues while at work. One of the quickest things that you can do to improve your communication through body language is to maintain eye contact while speaking with someone. Here are a few other tips and tricks for effectively using your body language.

- Keep an erect posture.
- While sitting, lean in towards someone

when speaking or listening to them.
- Be aware of how others are using their body language.
- Don't fidget.
- Be aware of cultural and gender differences.
- Keep an open and relaxed stance.
- Be conscious of your facial expressions.

With each message we send, there are both verbal and non-verbal cues. You should be practicing various forms of body language and ensuring that you are not coming off to other people as smug, arrogant or lacking confidence.

Being a better listener at work is all part of effective communication. Sometimes there might be a lot of environmental noise that you have to work through. However, if you take these tips into consideration, you should be able to effectively communicate in any work environment.

- Be quiet and let others speak without trying to come up with what you are going to say next.
- Repeat back to the person you are speaking with what you said in your own words.
- Maintain eye contact when the person is speaking, this will help you to retain information.
- Remember what someone is trying to say to you as if you will have to recall it later on.
- Minimize distractions from technology.
- Ask open-ended questions to clarify what was said.
- Be mentally and physically prepared to listen.
- Be present in the moment and listen.
- If you are unable to effectively hold a conversation with someone, schedule an appropriate time in the future.
- Ensure that your verbal and non-

verbal communication are cohesive.

Workplaces are becoming more and more diverse. It is vital to understand the importance of inclusivity in the workplace. It is a well-established fact that men and women communicate differently and gender stereotypes are inadvertently perpetuated by our everyday conversations. Effective communicators are able to hear facts and ideas and listen for the values and feelings behind them. Male leaders would benefit from specifically asking for input from their female counterparts.

Persuasive communication is also a very effective skill to have, particularly in the workplace. Knowing how to get people "on your side" so to speak, can help to influence people. People can be persuaded through likability, social proof, consistency, scarcity, authority and reciprocity. The more of one of these that you have, the more influence you hold over people. The effectiveness of your influence is not just about you, it is also dependent on your audience. Your audience needs to find your message relevant in order to be persuaded.

There are three main goals you should focus on when trying to persuade someone; affiliation, accuracy and positive self-concept. If you have some work to do to persuade people, then talking faster and repeating what you are saying will help people to believe in what you are saying. You also need to be sure that your audience is paying attention to what you are saying. When persuading people, you also need to be confident in your delivery.

When giving feedback, ensure that you are using "I" statements and framing the critique in a positive manner. It is also important to be able to self-critique and disarm your critics before they are able to start pointing fingers at what you have done wrong.

Employees who are proactive are able to

anticipate the needs of their team while being resourceful. Proactive employees are also not afraid to ask for help from their leadership team.

Coming up in the next chapter, you will learn how to effectively handle difficult situations and people in the workplace.

Chapter Three: How to Effectively Handle Difficult Situations and People in the Workplace

It happens in every workplace; there is at least one person that you work with who always seems to make things more difficult. At some point in your work career, you are going to work with difficult people or have to deal with difficult situations. It can be either internally or externally that you will experience difficult situations or people. However, that does not mean that it has to cause you a lot of stress or derail any of your goals.

How To Deal With Difficult People In Your Workplace; Coworkers or Customers

If you have ever worked in customer service, it is highly likely that you have had to deal with a difficult customer. In every workplace, there are going to be difficult people that you will have to work with. This might be clients, customers, vendors, colleagues or your leadership team (we will cover that next). Learning to deal with difficult people is a skill that is well worth spending time honing. While learning this skill can certainly be challenging, it can also prove to be very rewarding.

When you learn to deal with difficult people in your work environment, you can drastically improve employee morale and your satisfaction in the workplace (Heathfield, 2019). When you are able to address issues with a difficult coworker, it helps to create an overall better work environment. Difficult people in the work environment come in a wide variety but how you deal with them depends on you. It depends on your self-esteem, your self-confidence, your professional courage, as well as how often you have to work with that person.

It is generally easier to deal with a difficult person if other people in the workplace also find them difficult to work with. If that coworker is generally obnoxious or disliked, you can recruit other colleagues to help you address the situation. It might be wise to get your leadership team involved to help diffuse tense situations or when having to deal with difficult people. If you wait too long, things might spiral out of control and end up in a very negative situation. This could lead to the difficult person even undermining your professional credibility, attacking you and making you look bad.

You might even encounter situations at your work where you feel bullied. This can be outright and obvious or it can be much more subtle. You might work with a bully if you regularly feel intimidated or dread even going near that employee. Bullies tend to yell at other employees, insult them, put people down, physically or psychologically abuse or threaten people. Being bullied at work is not uncommon, it actually happens quite often. A bully might talk over you in meetings, regularly criticize your work or steal credit for your ideas or work performance.

Difficult people at work can also include those that are always negative. Some people, it doesn't matter what you do, they can just never seem to be positive. They always seem to be complaining about things, they don't like the company, they don't like their job and are just generally unpleasant to be around. Even while you practice positivity, it can be difficult to be around these people because they always seem to drag everyone down. Your best bet to deal with this kind of difficult person is to just avoid them altogether. If you can't avoid them and have to work with them at some point, then just do your best to remain positive.

There are many different types of difficult people that you can find in your workplace. Some of them just have a generally difficult personality while others seem to target you and your efforts. It doesn't really matter what kind of difficult person you are dealing with, it is not going to benefit you by simply avoiding them. You need to face the situation and handle it head-on. Most often, difficult people and situations become worse if left unaddressed.

You don't want to leave the issue of dealing with a difficult person unaddressed as it is only going to cause you anxiety and leave you miserable. You should not let others affect your attitude at work. If you are being treated in an unprofessional manner, do your best to understand why this is happening to you. You don't want to let your feelings fester and lead you to become irrational and thus react to this person in an unprofessional manner.

If you can avoid the person causing your stress at work, then do so. However, this is not always possible. If you complain about them to other coworkers this can quickly make you look like the bad guy (or girl) and you will be labeled as a whiner. Even if you have a manager or leadership team that is very understanding, they may begin to wonder why it is that you cannot solve your issues with said coworker yourself. If others feel that you are not able to handle difficult individuals at work then you too could quickly be labeled as a difficult person to work with. Not only is this a very troublesome title to get rid of, it can wreak havoc on your career.

In the event that there is someone you find difficult to work with, there are a few steps that you can take in order to clarify that is indeed the situation. Take some time to really consider if that person is actually the problem and it is not actually you. That is harsh to say, I know, but sometimes you are the problem and you don't even realize it. Talk with another trusted colleague to gauge their reaction to the person. See if you can approach the person you are having an issue with and see if you can speak with them about your issues. They might be doing something that they don't even realize they are doing. After you have spoken with them, has their behavior changed in any way? Has it gotten better or worse? Have they begun to single you out or do you find working with them enjoyable now?

You can also use humor to try and diffuse a tense situation. This is not effective for everyone. Some people are not naturally humorous and trying to be funny just might sound like making fun of the person. If being funny and joking does not come naturally to you, then don't do it.

On the chance that you have tried to deal with the difficult person on your own without success, it might be time to involve your leadership team. Don't address the issue as a personal problem that you have with that person, but rather an issue with productivity. Make sure to be specific and provide examples of how they are affecting your productivity. If you have separate managers, it is wise to include both party's bosses.

In the event that there are other individuals at work that are having issues with said employee, try to rally them together. This does not mean ganging up on them. This means taking the issues that you are all having with the person to your boss or to their boss. This might help to convince the leadership team that there really is an issue and it is not just one person picking on another.

How to Deal With a Difficult Boss at Work

Dealing with difficult bosses at work can be a whole other challenge. You can't take your issues to your boss because they are the one you are having issues with. It is bound to happen at some point that you will have to deal with a difficult boss in your work career. While it would be great if every boss that you have is trustworthy, competent, kind and fair, that is not likely the reality. A difficult boss can drastically affect employee engagement, productivity and the desire of employees to contribute to the team. Generally speaking, when an employee makes the decision to quit their job it is often due to their boss, not necessarily the company or the job itself. Having a boss that you can get along with is critical to employee satisfaction and retention.

It is unfortunate but sometimes when people are in a position of power they abuse that power and can become bullies to their employees. They may take credit for an employee's work, control them and never provide them with positive feedback. Just as with less than desirable coworkers, your boss might not realize that he is bad (Heathfield, 2018).

The undesirable qualities in your boss might come from a lack of training or micromanaging. Your boss might feel overwhelmed and not know how to give you the proper direction or support. If your boss was promoted too quickly, they might not realize their full responsibilities. Bosses from a different generation and different cultural backgrounds can also have conflicting views and cause friction in the workplace.

Try and resolve any issues you are having with

your boss by speaking with them first. Let them know what you need as far as direction, support and feedback are concerned. If you have access to another manager, seek out a mentor to help you figure out how to deal with your boss. Have a heart-to-heart with your manager and ask them how you can help them reach their goals. This can help them to realize that you want to help them and are willing to go the extra mile.

On the chance that speaking to your boss doesn't work, then you might need to go above his or her head and go to their boss or to human resources to resolve any issues. If you do go to your boss's boss or to human resources you might not fully ever find out what they did to resolve the issues, but you should at least give it some time to take effect. If there are other coworkers who have experienced your boss's unfair or rude behaviors, work with them collectively and visit human resources or their manager to discuss the situation.

What you need to realize from the start is that you have the right to work in a safe and professional environment. Don't get into any kind of public screaming match but try to draw his/her attention to his/her behavior privately when you have the opportunity. If you have made attempts to change without any success, then see if you are able to transfer departments.

How to Tactfully Handle Noisy and Disruptive Coworkers

You can't always choose your work environments or who is present in your work environment. You might unwillingly get stuck sitting by someone who is often loud and disruptive. Disruptive coworkers can not only wreak havoc on your productivity but also cause undue stress and tension in the workplace (Zenbooth, 2019). If you are dealing with a disruptive coworker, there are several things that you can do in order to tactfully handle any noisy and disruptive coworkers.

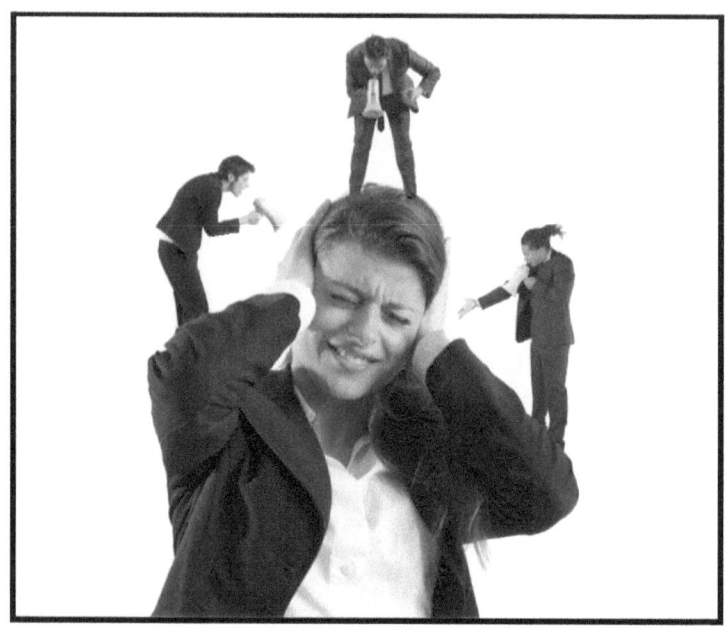

Try and handle the problem from your end. You might not realize it but some people are more sensitive to noise than others and if you are one of those people, someone that talks at a regular volume to others might feel overwhelming to you. If you are able to, bring a pair of noise-canceling headphones and listen to soothing music while you are by your noisy coworker. Just remember that you have headphones on before you start talking to someone else, you don't want to end up being the noisy coworker.

It is also in your interest to just be polite and ask if your coworkers are able to keep it down and explain why. Perhaps you need to take an important phone call or the like; it is a great excuse to communicate with your coworkers that work does not need to be loud. If you generally have a sense of humor, try making a cute or funny sign to cue to your colleagues to keep it down. However, this is only really a short-term solution if your coworkers are loud or noisy all of the time.

Generally speaking, if you are a rather polite person you can get away with simply asking others to keep quiet. Let them know that you really enjoy the fun work culture, but you just feel a little overwhelmed or distracted by how loud it can get at times. Hopefully, your colleagues are understanding and will work to keep the area around your workstation a little quieter. Unless your coworkers are just mean people or they don't like you for some reason, they should politely abide. You can also do your best to make it a two-way conversation and ask them if there is anything that you do that is disruptive to their work. This shows that you are also taking their productivity and workplace satisfaction into consideration.

You also have to be sure that you are not reinforcing the talkative or noisy behavior of your coworkers. If you have a coworker that is particularly talkative and they are consistently trying to talk with you, do your best to politely avoid them. When someone is being very talkative this is often attention-seeking behavior. If your chatty coworker continues to try and speak with you, respond to any questions they have with a short and to-the-point answer, then go back to what you were doing and divert your eye contact. This is a way to use your body language to let them know that the conversation is over. If they keep on trying to talk to you, just let them know that you have a lot of work to get finished and you are not trying to be rude but you need to focus on your task at hand.

Also make sure that you are setting a good example for your coworkers. If you are approached by a rather loud colleague, move the conversation somewhere where you will not disrupt other coworkers. If they don't want to move the conversation somewhere where they will not be disrupting others, simply ask them to lower their voice so as not to disturb those that are working. This should hopefully set an example for your loud coworkers.

If you are having difficulty with getting your coworkers to quiet down when you have to take an important call or need to get your work done, then scope out a quiet location. Most office buildings have spare conference rooms or empty offices that you can use either on a regular basis or on occasion for taking those important phone calls.

While going to your supervisor or human resources might be a last option, it might be your only option. Sometimes no matter how polite you are with your coworkers, there are some times where they just might not care about your work and would rather annoy you with their loud antics. It should always be the goal of human resources to provide everyone with a harmonious working environment. Human resources should be able to tactfully handle the situation and address it in a general manner rather than singling anyone out as being the loud one or the person making the complaint.

How to Manage Difficult Situations at Work and Keep Your Cool

It is one thing to deal with difficult people and bosses at work, it is another to deal with difficult situations. Difficult situations can arise with customers, with other coworkers, with vendors or your boss. Difficult situations at work, just as with difficult people, cause stress and anxiety.

Difficult work situations are caused by a lack of control. It might feel that everyone is out to get you and that there is nothing you can do about it. However, there are things that you can do about it!

Even if you are generally a level-headed person, your work environment can get the best of you. Bottling up all of your frustrations from work is not going to benefit anyone. It is likely that you will end up taking out your anger and frustrations on unwitting family members, like your kids or spouse. While we all know that exercise has many benefits, one more benefit is to be able to better handle difficult work situations. If you are able to squeeze in a brisk walk or quick run before headed out to work, this can not only provide you with mental clarity but also give you some energy for the day. You can easily release all the tension you are holding onto from work by working out for about 30 minutes per day. It might require you getting up a little bit earlier but I can promise you the benefits far outweigh the inconvenience of getting up a little earlier. When you have energy for the day and your mind is clear, you are able to focus better and not act irrationally to situations and be able to calmly deal with difficult work situations and coworkers.

It might also be beneficial to get an outside opinion of the situation. Overthinking situations can trap your mind in a continual downward spiral. It might feel like sometimes you can't escape your work life and that your entire life revolves around your work. It can become very overwhelming when the only point of view of the situation is your own. If you are finding your workplace difficult to deal with, then get out! Now, I am not saying that you should quit, what I am saying is that you should find a way to get out of work and to get your head out of work. Meet a friend who is not your coworker out for lunch or go for a walk. A friend that you do not work with might be able to offer an outside perspective on the situation. You can tell them exactly how you feel without having to worry about any backlash from your employer or coworkers.

Just as with overthinking things, it is possible to overanalyze your situation too. Much of the stress and anxiety about your work situation might stem from the feeling of just not being able to get out of the difficult situation. Your mind can be very powerful, in either a positive or negative light. It is easy to get caught up in the pattern of overthinking and trying to figure out everything that is going on at work, like who your boss is currently favoring or why you always seem to end up in difficult situations there. What you might not realize is that most of the situations are due to overthinking and are in your head. Most often these difficult working situations are not the actual reality but rather your mind running wild. Turn those negative thoughts about your work into actions. Focus on your work. Find a task within a project and throw yourself into it. Focus on making contributions to your workplace and gain back control over the situations you deal with at work (Miglani et al., 2019).

How to Overcome Your Coworkers' Poor Communication Skills

Even if you have become a first-class communicator in your workplace, it is unlikely that all of your coworkers will follow suit. While being able to communicate something to your team should seem like a simple process, there are any things that can interfere with getting the message across clearly.

There are certain ways to tell if you are working with a poor communicator. If the person you are speaking with doesn't seem to be communicating back to you or isn't giving you any feedback, it is likely that they are not great at communicating. This can also happen if you have a colleague who isn't getting any feedback either. They just might be talking too much and you should know by now that when it comes to effective communication you should be listening twice as much as you are talking.

You might also find that your coworker lacks

effective communication skills if they use "you" directives rather than "I" statements. For example, *"you never finish your part of the project on time."* An example of using an "I" statement would be something like; *"I feel like I am taking on more responsibility for the project."* Using "you" statements can make those people they are speaking with that they are being talked at rather than talked to. It might also feel that blame is being placed on them rather than having a neutral overtone. Do your coworkers react to ideas that are presented to them by shooting them down or do they engage in discussion about the idea? If they automatically shut down the idea then they are not very good communicators.

Poor communicators also don't really ever address the problem but rather the people. In addition to shooting down an idea they might also put down the people who presented the idea. An employee is never going to get positive results by spewing out negative comments to other coworkers. Individuals who are poor communicators also disregard or invalidate the feelings of their coworkers. They might also use passive-aggressive talk or sarcasm as a way of responding to professional and personal interactions.

You can work to overcome poor communicators by encouraging them to use effective communication skills. Don't play the blame game with them though, just provide them with a good example of effective communication and gently point out the things they could improve on.

How to Keep People from Wasting Your Time at Work

No matter who you are, time is your most precious commodity. In a work setting there are plenty of ways that people can waste your time, e.g. not showing up for a meeting (and not having the courtesy to cancel in advance) (Galek, 2019), stalling your work with their inability or disrupting your work in other ways. People can also waste your time by being time suckers. This can happen if you are an especially nice person who wants to help people; you can easily get taken advantage of. As a colleague and especially if you are a leader, there is a delicate balance between helping others and having your time wasted.

Time is precious; no one has unlimited time to be helping others, they generally have their own work to get done. You might think you are being helpful and responsive to your colleagues and their needs which of course is going to benefit the company, right? This is not always the case. You can't always say yes to every person every time. When your time is being taken up by someone or something else, you are not able to give your time to other more important people or tasks. If you have the same colleagues always coming to you for help on certain things, they can then learn to become dependent on you rather than trying to figure it out for themselves, which can become a vicious cycle. These colleagues are also wasting their own time by having to reach out to you all of the time and not being able to figure it out on their own. Perhaps instead of figuring out something on their own, they put it off until you can help them (Stachowiak, 2019). This can waste their time, yours and the company's.

While you want to be able to help your colleagues, there have to be rules and boundaries set in place to prevent people from wasting your time and to keep projects moving forward. Whether or not if you are a leader in your organization, it is not to say that you should always shut others out to avoid time wasters. You have to be smart about your time and how you spend it so that you aren't "busy" all day without actually getting anything done. Here are a few strategies to help you get more done during the day and ensure that you are also not feeling like you are blowing off your coworkers:

1) Try and book appointments with your coworkers (Stachowiak, 2019). This can work in two different ways. If you need to have a longer discussion with someone or if they need to have a longer discussion with you. If you are approached by a coworker and it is clear that their discussion with you is going to take more than five minutes, then you can book an appointment with them to fully discuss the issue at hand. I'm sure you have dealt with people like this before; they say it's only going to take a few minutes, but in reality, it takes much longer. Setting an appointment will not only benefit you but also will benefit them. When you have time to have a discussion you are

able to be present for it rather than thinking about when this person is going to stop talking. Making an appointment with someone to discuss an issue allows both parties to get all of their questions answered fully and be able to focus on the most important factors of the discussion.

2) If someone seems to keep coming to you for little things here and there throughout the day, have them make a list. When they think of something they need to discuss with you, have them write it down either on a piece of paper or in a shared document. If the discussion is not urgent then you should be able to access their list and set an appointment to have a discussion about things with them. This works well because you can send them a meeting agenda in advance to make sure they will have all of their questions answered.

3) When you do set a meeting or appointment with someone, make sure you are setting a time limit and sticking to it! While setting a meeting

can help to avoid wasting time, this can also backfire on you. If you set a meeting for 30 minutes, and 90 minutes later you are still discussing topics, this defeats the purpose of having a meeting set in the first place. If you are part way through the meeting and you realize that it is going to take a lot longer to resolve the issues at hand, then set up another time to talk. A tactic that you can use to make sure that your meetings don't run over is to book another appointment right after so that you are obligated to end the meeting on time.

4) Make sure you are asking questions to help your colleagues to try and solve their own problems. While it can feel great when others come to you for answers, people need to figure out how to solve their own problems. Just giving people the answers all of the time is not going to help them in the long run and is only going to make them dependent on you. Don't just do other people's work for them. Even if you are not technically a leader within your organization, you

can still act like a leader and possess leadership qualities. You can provide coaching or mentoring to colleagues, but don't just do their work and give them all the answers.

5) When it comes to not giving people all the answers, you also have to be sure that you are helping them to come up with solutions as well. Sometimes people just need to vent, and that is ok. However, the conversation you are having should be focused on finding solutions rather than simply complaining or venting. If you and your colleague are unable to come up with a solution, ask them to schedule another appointment with you when they have found a solution to the problem. This can be difficult at first, but this signals to your coworkers that you are serious about your time and are not going to wait around for them to come and complain to you.

Chapter Summary

Regardless of the workplace, you are bound to run into difficult people and or situations. Whether you are dealing with clients, customers or vendors, there are bound to be difficult situations that arise and difficult people that you have to work with. When you are able to handle difficult people in a tactful manner, you will improve your overall morale and workplace satisfaction. When you regularly practice positivity at work, you cancel out others' negativity and are able to defend yourself from their negative ways. While it is ideal that you avoid difficult people altogether, this might not always be an option. In the worst-case scenario, you will have to recruit your management team or human resources to help resolve a difficult issue or to deal with a difficult person.

In the unfortunate circumstance that you get stuck with a very difficult boss, you can always take the route of "killing them with kindness".

However, having a difficult boss can make a work situation very distressing as you might have to go above their heads to their boss or human resources. So often people quit a job they love or a company that they enjoy working for just because the person they report directly to is very difficult to work with. Unfortunately, people in positions of power can abuse that position, causing distress and frustration among their team.

You might also run into the problem of having to deal with noisy and disruptive coworkers, especially if you do not have your own office. It is best to handle these people and situations with rapport and humor when possible. Ensure that you are setting a good example for your coworkers and scoping out quieter locations if necessary.

Dealing with difficult situations at work can lead to high levels of stress and anxiety. Anxiety-ridden work environments can get the best of even the most level-headed individuals. Do your best to stay focused on your work and making positive contributions to your organization.

If you have been really practicing your effective communication skills, it is likely that you will begin to realize how ineffective other people's communication skills are. You can encourage your colleagues to brush up on their communication skills by using "I" statements, giving positive feedback and addressing the problem rather than the person or people involved in the problem.

Another very large issue that can often arise at work is other people wasting your time. If you have a colleague who is constantly asking you for a few minutes of your time that then turns into 45 to 60 minutes, ask them to schedule a meeting with you so that you may discuss all of their concerns. You can also have your colleague make a list of things that they would like to discuss with you in order to speed up your interaction and address all of their concerns. Don't forget to stick to your meeting times and don't let your coworkers bully you into wasting your time to fill their needs.

In the next chapter, you will learn tips and tricks on how to be the most effective leader you can be.

Chapter Four: How to Be The Most Effective Leader You Can Be

What does being an effective leader mean to you? Businesses are built on successful leadership. Leaders need to be flexible and able to easily adapt to situations (Daskal, 2019). Leaders also need to be able to delegate tasks effectively. An effective leader also needs to be charismatic as well as an effective communicator. Leaders should be able to set goals effectively and help to move their teams forward by inspiring and leading with a shared vision. And of course, be able to take action!

How to Become a More Charismatic Leader

When you think of someone who is charismatic, who comes to mind? Winston Churchill, Richard Branson?

Often times people think that being charismatic is something that someone is born with. However, you can learn to be charismatic with a little practice. Leaders that are charismatic are influential, persuasive and inspire others. People are drawn to charismatic people; they want to be part of their circle of influence, they want to learn from you (Giang, 2019). Charismatic leaders don't require a long list of qualifications or education to qualify them as credible.

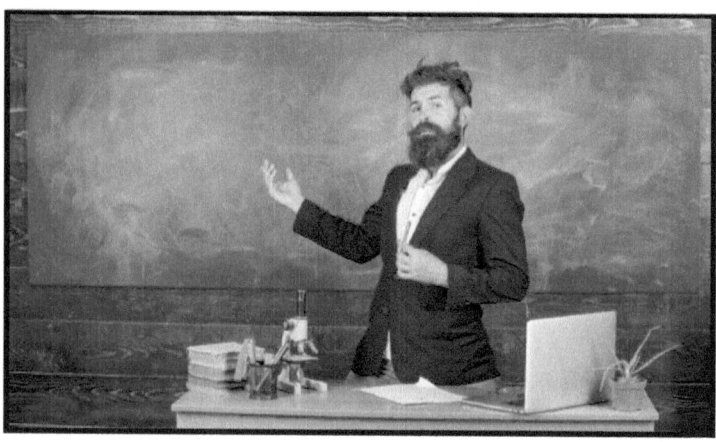

Someone who is charismatic knows how to make others feel that they are intelligent, impressive and fascinating (Giang, 2012). People who are charismatic have a way of uplifting others and making them feel good about themselves. Charismatic leaders are present with their audience. You can pause before answering or asking questions of those you are speaking with. Don't just be waiting for someone to finish what they are saying before you start talking and thinking about your rebuttal in the meantime. Make sure your face is showing some type of interest and you aren't sitting there with a blank stare on your face - this is not going to win you any fans.

There are several things that you can do if you would like to become a more charismatic leader. First, you have to build a connection with your audience. Some leaders choose to lead just by using their authority; this leaves your colleagues and those employees that report to you feeling like you are the boss and they have to remain under your command. Charismatic leaders are able to connect with people on various levels, sometimes even on a personal level. Talk to people and get to know them. People love to talk about themselves or their kids. It is also beneficial to ask for your colleagues' input. Don't just spew off your demands and expect people to follow along. Ask them their opinions and if they feel things are headed in the right direction. Doing this on an occasional basis will let your team members know that their leader is there to do more than just lead them, their leader is there to listen to them and learn from them.

Charismatic leaders put people at ease and don't make their audience or colleagues feel too serious. Charismatic leaders squash tension with light humor while still ensuring that their team remains productive. While it is a delicate balance, a good and charismatic leader is able to maintain a balance between being too serious and being too easygoing. As a charismatic leader, you are able to share stories that show your vulnerability and that you are indeed human. Leaders who possess a lot of confidence and are very likable are often seen as charismatic. Charisma is also a quality that people who are able to sway individuals with their arguments to their point of view possess. With great confidence also comes great humility and a charismatic leader will understand that they are not the smartest person in the room. This helps to bring confidence to the team and to the individuals on the team by empowering them.

Trustworthiness and not going back on their promises is also another trait of charismatic leaders. There is nothing worse than a leader who says they are going to do one thing and ends up doing something else and breaking the trust of their team. Charismatic leaders also have a very strong commitment to their goals and lead by example. They don't mind being in the trenches with their team and are in it to get the job done! They are also able to motivate their team to get done what they need to get done.

The Essentials to Becoming a Master

Communicator

With any business, learning to become a master communicator is key. Just as with any skill, you can learn to communicate effectively with a few simple tactics. First of all, you need to discover your own individual voice. Everyone has a different personality and how you interact and speak with people will set you apart from others. Other people will recognize you from your voice, your tone and how you verbally carry yourself (Adams, 2019). Stand out without being arrogant or obnoxious.

Mastering communication also requires confidence. Confidence portrays that you understand what you are talking about and are able to communicate your message to others. Even if you are generally introverted, you can still speak with confidence. People you are speaking with are able to tell if you are confident in what you are saying or if you are just trying to avoid looking like a fool. No matter the situation you find yourself in, you should remain confident.

When you are communicating with others, you should not worry about speaking fast but rather slow down a bit. Those that you are communicating with need to be able to understand what you are saying. Speaking fast is not necessary in most cases and can actually lead to miscommunication. Your communications should also have a purpose (Adams, 2019). You should be able to share your message with others in an effective manner by portraying a clear focus.

Master communicators are also able to engage with their audience. Being a master communicator isn't always about the person who is speaking, it is also about the people or person they are speaking to. Engaging with people, saying their names, making eye contact, shaking hands and so on lets them know that you care about your message and how they are receiving the message.

How Leaders Effectively Set Goals

Whether you are an employee who is striving to be a leader or you are already leading a team, setting goals within your organization is important. Goal setting as a leader can be even more important as you are not only setting goals for yourself but also for those on your team. Just as with many other goals in life, you should set S.M.A.R.T. goals and make them simple, measurable, achievable, realistic, and time bound. These goals are ones that you can set by yourself or with your team. You should focus on no more than five for the next 12 months and they should be very clear (Peck, 2017).

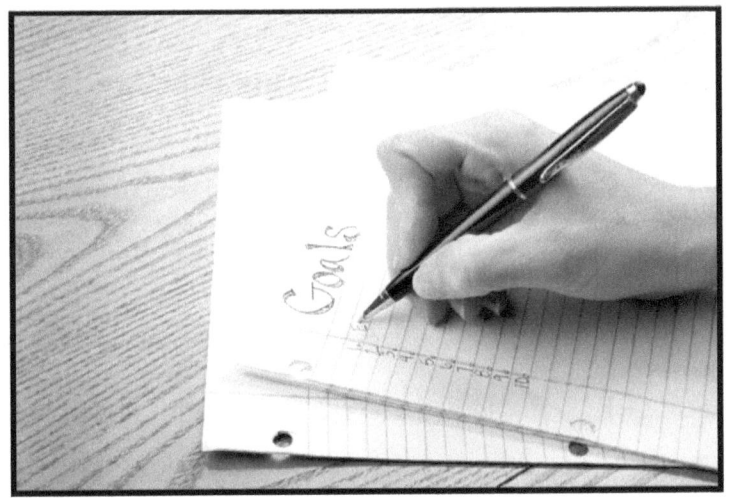

Goal setting is important to leaders for several reasons. Goal setting shows that you as the leader are competent in achieving performance results. Setting and achieving goals with your team instills confidence in you and themselves. When you see that they can set and achieve targeted results they will want to keep going with achieving more goals.

When you set goals for your team, it helps to give each person direction. Each individual involved should understand their part in the goal and target their efforts to achieve the goal. When you, as a leader, set goals and your team works to achieve them, this is also letting you assess their abilities at the same time. Goal setting and achieving also shows ownership of goals and projects.

S.M.A.R.T. goals are always the safest way to set goals either by yourself or when working with a team. Remember that your S.M.A.R.T. goals should be specific, measurable, achievable, results-oriented, and timebound. You cannot say, "let's get more clients!" and use that as a goal. A S.M.A.R.T. goal for getting more clients would be something like: "Make X# of outbound sales calls per day, follow up with X# of current clients and work to obtain X# of sales per week/day." While not all of your goals will be completely in your hands and might depend on outside factors (like clients), having a S.M.A.R.T. goal helps to make those goals specific and easy for everyone to understand.

In addition to focusing on S.M.A.R.T. goals, you also have to realize that there are two different types of goals, performance and learning. Performance goals focus on specific end goals and results, such as getting more clients or building a new prototype. Learning goals focus on creativity and expending on skill development, such as increasing your emotional intelligence or other soft skills. Whenever possible, get the people on your team to help with goal setting. Generally speaking, when someone helps to build their goal they are going to be more committed to it.

How to Clarify Your Values at Work

Your values are things that you should adhere to both inside and outside of work. They are beliefs and ideas that you have identified as core principles and are an integral part of who you are. Your values can be things like honesty, humility, self-respect, respecting others or success (however you may define that). Before you ever choose your career and/or accept a job, you should have your values defined. Don't worry, it's not too late to start defining your values.

There are two different types of values, intrinsic and extrinsic (Rosenberg McKay, 2018). The intrinsic values, when it comes to establishing values at work, are those that have to do with the actual work tasks performed. Examples of intrinsic values result in job satisfaction and engagement. The extrinsic values are the results of the by-products of your job. This has to deal with what you get out of your work, not what you put into it. Extrinsic values include things like your salary, job security and recognition.

While it is good practice to identify your work values very early on in your work career, it is not too late to identify them now. There is a simple inventory that you can do to access your work values in which you define them and number them from one to ten. This is called a work values inventory (Rosenberg McKay, 2018). Write down ten of your values and number them from one to ten with one being the most important and ten being the least important. While you can recruit a professional to do a work values inventory with you, you can also complete one easily on your own. Even though you might stay within the same occupation, various jobs require various values. If you value working with others, a job with a lot of autonomy is probably not going to fit well with your values.

If you are having difficulty coming up with some workplace values then here is a list of a few to get you started:

- Achievement
- Recognition
- Independence
- Relationships
- Support
- Autonomy
- Working conditions
- Helping others
- Prestige

- Collaboration
- Job security
- Salary or compensation
- Using your skills or background
- Leadership
- Influence
- Creativity
- Variety
- Challenging
- Opportunities
- Leisure
- Artistic or creative expression

While defining your values is important, you should not isolate them from other factors of your work life, such as your personality, abilities or aptitudes and interests.

How to Find Your Voice at Work and Use It!

For many, speaking up at work can be a challenge. Some very bright, smart, opinionated people with great ideas are left silent due to a fear or an internal battle that is keeping them quiet. People might have their voice at work stifled by intimidation, lack of respect, fear of rejection, fear of confrontation, not wanting to draw attention to themselves, being afraid of looking stupid or that no one will listen to them even if they do try and speak (Scivique, 2010).

Having a voice at work is important because you deserve it! When you share your thoughts with your leadership team or with your colleagues, it shows that you are engaged in your work. It should, as long as you are engaging with a positive voice, bring positive attention your way. You will earn more respect from your colleagues and your management team. Your work will become more stimulating as you become more involved. Furthermore, you learn more! When you become engaged with your work, your leadership team will take notice and you should have access to more opportunities within your workplace. There are a few things that you can do in order to find your voice in the workplace and start using it so others will notice you in a positive way.

In order to find your voice, you need to practice many of the skills needed to become a good communicator. You first need to learn to listen. You need to really listen to what others are saying before speaking up or giving your opinion. You want your contribution to be helpful and not hinder the conversation. Nor do you want to distract or be off-topic. You also need to be selective in what you are saying. If you just spout off your opinion about everything that everyone has to say then they are going to stop listening to you.

You should always be sure that you are picking the right time and place to use your voice. Take note of what is going on around you before you just start to talk about things. If there is high tension in the room, you might want to wait until a different time to speak with someone or ask to have a private conversation instead. If you have something important to say, a noisy room full of people might not be the best place or time.

All business conversations should have a professional tone, with a neutral and non-judgmental language. If you are talking in a tone that is making people feel attacked, then they are likely to shut down and become defensive. Using your polite voice and basic social etiquette can go a long way.

While it would be great if your colleagues and leadership team listened to you just because you are you, that is not a likely scenario. Although you deserve to be heard, sometimes you really need to show people proof. Proof that what you are saying is valid or that is it going to work the way you say it is going to work. Collect data to support your idea and present people with facts whenever possible. Even though you might trust your gut, it is unlikely that others are going to trust in your gut. And overall, avoid being a chatterbox. While it is great to be able to express your opinions and ideas, speak in a clear and concise manner. Give your thoughts a voice and then stop talking. You need to give others time to reflect on what you have said and then ask them for their thoughts and feedback.

Leadership Tips to Inspire a Shared Vision

A shared vision is similar to a goal. It is defined with an end goal in mind in which the team works together on objectives to achieve that vision. Inspiring a shared vision helps employees to see the deeper meaning in their work rather than just doing the daily grind. There are two main things that leaders can do to help inspire a vision of the future; define the vision and bring along others by working toward the vision of the future (Mugavin, 2019).

In order to inspire a vision for the future, look at the past and present goals of the organization and how these can help to inform the vision of the future of the organization. Get your colleagues and team members involved in the process and ask them about their goals and aspirations and how they can fit into the larger organizational goals. Focus on how the team's or organization's shared vision will help them to achieve their individual goals. And don't forget to regularly check in with your team to see how the progress on the shared vision is coming along.

When you are regularly checking in with your team about your shared vision, make sure to reflect on what has worked, what has not worked and what you could do differently.

- How do your colleagues and team members talk about their vision for the future?
- What are the big picture goals for the team?
- How does each individual person fit into the vision for the future?
- How can I, as a leader, include others to be part of this vision for the future?

- Do we as a team think about the future often enough?

Having a shared vision makes you, as a leader, a visionary.

How to Be a Great Leader and Take Action

We often put leaders up on a pedestal without realizing all the difficult decisions they might have to make. We see leaders as having all of the answers, but what we don't realize is the huge mistakes that they can make and the costly failures they might have made in the past. We often think leadership is effortless and comes naturally to people, when in fact, being a leader is no accident. Leaders need to be prepared and tough when it comes to making decisions (Whalen, 2018). It really doesn't matter what decision you make, there is always going to be someone that is unhappy about it.

Setting the table for success is something that

leaders excel at. They get an agreement from their employees, upfront, to be able to hold them accountable. This lets people know in advance that they will be called out if they are not pulling their weight. Leaders that take action don't always treat everyone the same, but they do always treat everyone with respect, even if they don't necessarily deserve it. Leaders are there to help every employee reach their potential but not necessarily to help them get to the top of the organization.

Leaders who take action and get results are always coaching their employees. They need to be able to know how to maximize their time effectively and to the best of their abilities. With coaching others, you need to also have a high level of humility. If, you the leader, does something wrong you need to be the first to admit it and take responsibility for your actions.

In addition, leaders that take action also know the importance of self-improvement, personal and professional development. Being a leader is not a destination but rather a journey. As a leader you affect other people in ways that you may not realize can have a lasting impact. If you don't get enough sleep and are crabby to one of your employees, they might become stressed and mess up something within your project. So, as a leader you need to take care of yourself and realize that your actions and attitude go far beyond just you.

There are so many famous leaders and innovators that just didn't know how to give up and therefore learned from their past mistakes. There is a famous quote by Thomas Edison, "I have not failed. I've just found 10,000 ways that won't work." This really embodies the concept that people should be able to learn from their mistakes and use that to create a better work environment and build better quality leadership skills.

Great leaders who take action are also empathetic and get their team's input before they make decisions. Employees lose trust in their leadership team when things change and they seemingly have no control over it, such as compensation plans or changes to a project. Including your team in the decision-making process can go a long way in building trust with your team. This way when you do have to make decisions without consulting them first, they will trust in your decision.

A good leader should be able to take action and seek out individuals to give increasing responsibility to. When team members are empowered, they will go above and beyond what they are asked to perform to meet expectations. Leaders also ask for feedback when they take actions. When leaders take action they also need humility in order to gracefully receive criticism from their team members.

Lastly, leaders need to be prepared to take action and then get out of the way! Taking action also means realizing that you don't have all the answers and that some people are better equipped to do certain things than you are.

Chapter Summary

Everyone is captivated by a great leader; someone who is charismatic, who can easily sway people to their point of view and who can awe an audience, leaders that are charismatic are able to influence, persuade and inspire their team members. There are several things that you can do if you want to become a charismatic leader:

- Build a connection with your audience.
- Be trustworthy and uphold your promises.
- Show humility and vulnerability.
- Put your audience at ease.
- Connect with your audience at various levels.
- Maintain a delicate balance between serious and easygoing.
- Be confident without being arrogant.

- Understand that you are not the smartest person in the room.
- Show your strong commitment to your goals and lead by example.
- Be in the trenches with your team and get things done.

When you have become a master communicator, you can communicate with a distinct voice that others will recognize. Make eye contact, shake hands and let others know that you care about the message that you are sending.

Leaders are also well versed in setting goals both for themselves and for their teams. They work on establishing S.M.A.R.T. goals, meaning they are specific, measurable, achievable, results-oriented and timebound. Great leaders are also aware of the different types of goals, the performance and learning.

Great leaders also have clearly defined values and consistently work towards them. It is ideal that you have your values clearly defined before you go out and look for a job, but it is never too late to start defining your values for work now. Common workplace values include achievement, independence, support, autonomy and influence.

For many people, speaking up is challenging. But just remember that you have a voice and you deserve to be heard. When you voice your concerns it shows that you are engaged with your work and aren't afraid to bring positive attention your way. Before you find your voice, you need to make sure that you are listening, you want to make sure that you are contributing rather than hindering the process. You also have to be selective about the time and the place that you are using your voice. Any and all conversations related to business should have a professional tone and ensure basic social etiquette.

Leaders should also be able to inspire a shared goal. They can do this by getting their colleagues and team members involved in the process.

When you are checking in with your team about your shared vision, always make sure that you positively reflect on the work that they have done together.

Finally, great leaders are those that are able to take action without sacrificing their integrity. Being a leader is no easy trip and great leaders don't just happen by accident. Great leaders are always checking in with and coaching their employees to reach their fullest potential.

In the next chapter, I will focus on the most common communication mistakes and how to avoid them.

Chapter Five: The Most Common Communication Mistakes and How to Avoid Them

You should already know that communication is at the core of everything and all relationships. In order to build better communication skills, you should also be aware of the most common mistakes and how to avoid them.

Think about the people that you admire, the great leaders, speakers and entrepreneurs; one thing that most of them have in common is their ability for effective communication. There are many things that you can do to ensure that you are being an effective communicator, making sure that you are listening before you are talking, repeating back to the person what they said in your own words, so on and so forth. But what are the things that you shouldn't do? There are many mistakes that people can make in their communication that can lead to confusion and frustration.

Communication is not a one-size-fits-all approach. When speaking with a group of people, some will understand what you are saying, while others might need further explanation. You can avoid miscommunication with a larger audience by first considering the people you are speaking with and their learning styles. Make your communication strategy one that will appeal to all those you are communicating with.

Another very common communication mistake is a lack of attention to your tone of voice. You might need to adjust your tone of voice based on who you are talking to or the situation you are finding yourself in. Before you start to speak, whether you are in a large group or in a one to one conversation, take a breath and access your tone.

People often think they are effectively communicating if they avoid difficult conversations and situations. This is not true. Everyone faces a conflict at some point in their workplace. However, simply avoiding the conflict does not make it go away. If you need to have a difficult conversation with someone, then prepare for it. Write down a list of clear and positive feedback if you have to and always try and end on a positive note.

Poor communicators often hold back what they are truly thinking about. Being a good communicator is about stating what you need in a tactful manner and still being able to understand the needs of others. A good communicator is able to speak clearly while making their requests known without jeopardizing the relationship with the person they are speaking with.

When someone reacts to a situation rather than responds to it, this also shows poor communication skills. When you react to a situation you show anger, frustration, and might be impulsive. When something happens that you feel the urge to react to, take a deep breath and stop before you do anything. First you must understand the facts of the situation, don't jump to conclusions and make assumptions about the situation.

A very big communication mistake is indulging in gossip. It's unfortunate, but it happens. Gossip can ruin people's reputations and drastically break down trust in relationships. Even gossip that is not intended to hurt others can have devastating consequences. As a trusted and effective communicator you should not give in to gossip and you should leave no room for innuendo or speculation.

Close-minded people can make some very big miscommunication mistakes. Today's work environments are becoming more and more diversified. Don't be close-minded about anyone but rather open your mind and your heart to embrace diversity. Embracing diversity allows you to communicate with people who have a range of diverse experiences and creativity which can ultimately be beneficial.

I mentioned this point previously; you have two ears and one mouth, so you should not be speaking more than you are listening. Unless someone has hired you to give a speech - that is a little different. People often think communication is a one-way street and they do all of the talking and very little listening. Don't be that person! If you want to really understand what is going on to be able to effectively communicate, you need to listen to what is going on. This encourages learning and shows empathy to the person you are communicating with.

Lastly, and probably one of the worst communication mistakes, is when you assume you are being understood. This can cause a miscommunication domino effect. You think you are being understood, you give everyone the go ahead to work on what they need to work on, then it all comes crashing down, but you can't seem to figure out why. You made the mistake by making the assumption that everyone understood what they needed to do. You need to check in with people to ensure that they understood your message rather than assuming that they understood it (Daskal, 2014).

There are many ways that you can be misunderstood and make communication mistakes. However, if you are aware of what they are, you can recognize them and work to avoid them.

Chapter Summary

In order to master the skill of communication, you should also be aware of the potential communication mistakes and how to avoid them. Effective communication is not a one-size-fits-all approach. Here are some of the most common forms of miscommunication:

- Lack of attention to your tone of voice.
- Avoiding rather than facing conflict.
- Not speaking clearly while making a request.
- Jumping to conclusions without getting the facts first.
- Indulging in gossip.
- Being close-minded.
- Speaking more than listening.
- Thinking that someone understands you when they don't.

The next chapter will focus on expert tips and tricks for effective communication in the workplace.

Chapter Six: Expert Tips and Tricks for Effective Communication in The Workplace

Now that you are aware of all the mistakes that you can make when communicating, how can you become an expert communicator? When you can effectively communicate with your team members and with your leadership team, you will help to eliminate any misunderstandings and encourage a healthy and peaceful work environment (Belonwu, 2018).

We communicate every day and in many ways. However, being able to effectively communicate at work takes some additional finesse (Watson, 2019). You need to be able to shut off your mind and not think about what you are going to say next but rather fully listen to your colleagues and choose the right words and tone to respond with.

The repercussions of miscommunication in the workplace can be far more serious; resulting in loss of employee motivation, poor productivity and an overall breakdown in communication among team members. Here are nine expert tips and tricks for effective communication in the workplace.

First, you need to be diplomatic when you handle conflicts. Conflict can easily arise when people are working together all day long and working against deadlines. Conflicts can result from silly things like someone not changing the printer ink, or from major things like taking credit for someone else's work. Even small and minor issues can turn into much larger disputes. In order to prevent smaller issues from developing into larger issues, get control of them right away. Encourage employees on your team to come to you and let them know that your door is always open. Make sure that you are creating an environment that is comfortable and makes your employees feel safe by ensuring confidentiality.

Being diplomatic about the conflict means keeping an open mind and not being judgmental. You are not attacking people or placing blame on anyone but rather asking questions to get to the bottom of things. You should be able to find a solution that is acceptable for everyone.

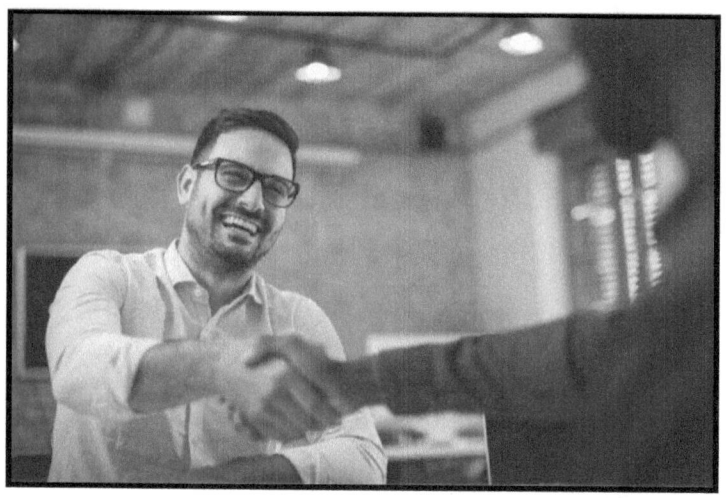

There are too many conversations that take place in companies that are a result of email or other technologies. Emails and instant messages are sent to colleagues that you are sitting right next to with a simple cubicle wall in between. Don't forget the art of the simple conversation. Stop relying on your computer so much and resurrect the art of the conversation. While the technology that we use can be very beneficial in speeding up your communications, it can lose its real communicative effect. You also lose out on the non-verbal cues of the communication such as tone and body language. Miscommunications can increase even more when the sender or the receiver of the message does not take their time or is not articulate.

Effective communicators are able to respect cultural differences when they are communicating with others in the workplace. Simple hand symbols or gestures that might be harmless to some cultures could be extremely offensive to other cultures. Many companies hire employees that come from different cultures to work directly in their offices or virtually. As a result, team members and management teams need to be aware of the cultural sensitivities. These can be subtle differences, such as words and gestures, or very blatant differences. The company itself needs to create an environment that is conducive to cultural inclusivity. This can include things like offering specific types of foods in the cafeteria, allowing days off for certain religious holidays and providing training to other employees about being culturally sensitive.

Those individuals that are effective communicators are able to provide good feedback to their employees and team members. Whether you are a leader or a colleague, it is important to let your colleagues know that they are doing well. It increases motivation when an employee's efforts are recognized. Holding regular meetings is a great way to provide employees with feedback, but you don't need to save your feedback and encouragement just for meetings. You can send them a quick email, text or give them a quick call to get a status report and give them your feedback. Ensure that your feedback is clear and concise and that you're able to offer a solution to any difficulties that they might be struggling with (Watson, 2019).

You need to trust in your people! Being a micromanager is not fun for anyone. When you micromanage your employees they lose motivation because they then feel like they can't do anything right when you are consistently hovering over them. As a leader you hired competent employees that should be able to own their own work. As an effective communicator you should be able to communicate to your employees what they need to do and just periodically check in to make sure they don't need your assistance.

Companies that are built on trust actually listen to their employees. When employees are communicated with and feel like owners they will have a higher emotional stake in the company. Transparency is a critical part of the employees taking ownership of the company and their projects. There are very few companies that truly practice transparency and reveal things like their costs and profits. When employees really feel that they are part of the company and that they are part owners, they are more committed and produce more results.

Leaders and employees who can effectively communicate are able to take their emotions out of the communication equation. It can be difficult to professionally communicate in the workplace when there are clashing personalities that you work with. It's unfortunate, but it happens; an argument at work can quickly turn into a personal attack. Before you escalate a situation by reacting to it, stop, take a breath and count down from ten if you need to, then calmly respond without being emotional about it. Don't take other people's reactions personally. Use your "I" statements and don't place blame on others, rather give them suggestions. Be sure that the person you are communicating with is understanding what you are communicating to them and not taking something in the wrong way. Ask them for clarification or feedback on what you talked about together.

Great communicators ensure that they are fully listening when in a conversation rather than just hearing what the other person is saying. It happens to the best of us and that is ok. You are speaking with someone and before you know it, they have had a whole conversation with you and you have no idea what you talked about. Make sure as an effective communicator, that you are actually listening to what the person is saying. Actually listening to someone is much more difficult than it sounds. If you are having difficulty effectively listening in a conversation, pretend you will be tested on what was said. Make a checklist in your head that focuses on the important points in the conversation then recall those points after the conversation has ended. You can also repeat back to the person what they said in your own words to ensure that you have accurately heard what they have said.

Lastly, ensure that your work environment is fun (Watson, 2019)! This might sound a little weird to talk about having fun when talking about communication, however, the two are interconnected. When companies give employees the chance to have fun, they are communicating to them that they appreciate their hard work and efforts.

Chapter Summary

Once you have become aware of all of the various ways you can ineffectively communicate with someone in the workplace, it's time to focus on all of the ways you can effectively communicate with people.

- Shut off your mind and focus on the conversation at hand.
- Be diplomatic when handling conflict.
- Minimize the use of technology in conversations.
- Respect cultural differences.
- Provide good and positive feedback to employees and colleagues.
- Trust in your people.
- Take emotion out of the communication equation.
- Use your "I" statements.
- Ensure everyone is having fun!

Finally, in the bonus chapter we will discuss how

to become a master at public speaking and why you need this skill to be effective in the workplace.

Bonus Chapter: How to Become a Master at Public Speaking

Now, you might be wondering why a book on effective communication in the workplace would have a chapter on how to become a master at public speaking. Even if you are not a "public speaker," public speaking is a skill that anyone can master. Many, many people are afraid of public speaking and are therefore not very good at it. It doesn't really matter if you are speaking to a group of investors or just a room full of your colleagues, mastering public speaking can be a big key to success. Learning to give a good presentation is a coachable skill that anyone can learn. With that in mind, let's take a look at how to become a master of public speaking, even if the thought of it currently makes you feel like throwing up.

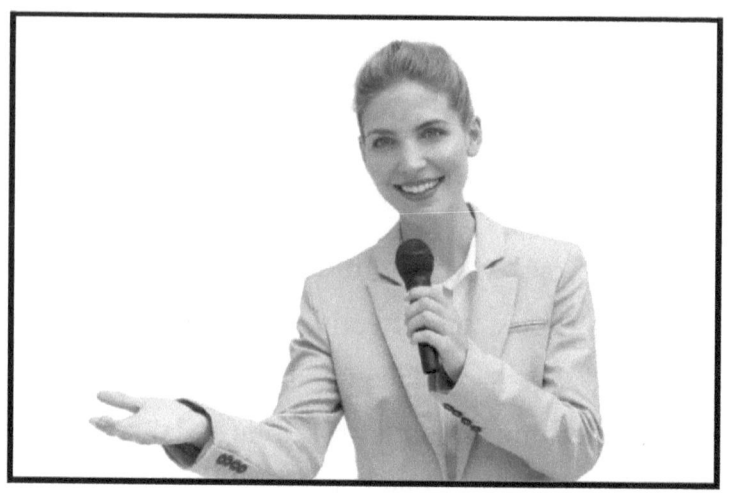

The very first step is to not get too technical. You really have to consider the audience that you are speaking to. While you might be an expert in quantum mechanics, your audience might not be as well versed in all the technical nuances. Your speech or conversation should start where your audience is (Kapla, 2016), not where you are. If you are giving a speech or having a conversation, think of it like a journey. Where is your audience starting at? How did they get there? Where do you want to take them? And how will you get there?

One key factor to a great presentation is to brighten someone's day or to leave them with something. You should be able to give your audience something that they can take away from the conversation or speech. This can be some actionable advice or a feeling or confidence. Before you start your speech or conversation, think about ways that you can improve your audience's day and go from there.

Something that people greatly underestimate is the importance of practice when public speaking. Once you figure out what you want to say, you need to figure out how you are going to say it. There are three main ways to deliver a speech; you can write it down and read a script, summarize your main ideas into bullet points or memorize the entire thing. While reading from a script can be very effective in delivering your message, it is not so great for your audience. People can tell when you are reading from a script and quickly become disinterested. Your best bet is to memorize your entire speech. If you practice, practice, practice, you should be able to memorize your speech with only having to occasionally look at your notes and be able to deliver a speech that keeps your audience engaged and keeps you in the flow.

Be highly aware of your body language. When people first begin public speaking, they are very often unaware of what to do with their bodies, which can lead to unnecessary fidgeting and body movements. Learning the skill of public speaking is like taking baby steps to work towards becoming a professional. When you are speaking you should be standing still and just using your hand gestures to emphasize your points rather than shifting your weight from side to side or swaying. You also need to ensure that you are taking out your filter words; "like," "um," and "ya' know," are some of the most commonly used.

With great public speaking, less is more. While using slides or other multimedia can help to get your point across or further explain complex subjects, your slides should not be used as a substitute for your bulleted notes. Furthermore, do not read from your slides and put the same information in your slides that you are saying - that is redundant, your audience can read.

Great public speakers are always honing their craft and welcome feedback and constructive criticism (Kaplan, 2016). While you are practicing your speech, ask your friends or family for feedback. You might be surprised at what you learn. You can also film yourself to study your body language, tone of voice and cadence when speaking.

With any speech, it should not only give your audience something, but also give your listeners a reason to care. Your speech or conversation should not be all about you but rather the speech should be thought of as a two-way conversation. Is what you are talking about something you would like to hear about? If you are having this conversation or pitching something to someone, don't do a hard sell. If what you are selling is of value to the person, they will naturally want to buy from you.

We each have two different voices; our best voice which is our most confident, and our insecure voice. Our insecure voice tends to come out when we are talking about things we are not very sure or confident about. These might be things that we have little knowledge in or that we are not confident in having the answer to. Your best voice is your most confident voice. It might be where you find humor in things or when you are speaking about a subject that you are very passionate and knowledgeable about. With your best voice you light up and could talk forever about a subject.

You must also consider your style of speaking when speaking with others (Lear, 2019). Public speaking skills that you learn can be used either in a group setting, such as a large presentation, or in small and intimate settings like a one-on-one sales call. You can either stay true to your style of speaking, which might be calm and collected or excited and full of energy, or you might match the other person's style of speaking. Some people become very overwhelmed when they are speaking with someone on the phone and they are speaking very fast and are full of energy while other people might then come to up to that level and match their excitement. This is one of those situations where you really have to read your audience and determine what is going to get you the best results.

If public speaking is a skill that you truly want to master, then you need to practice and put in the work. The first big step is practicing; practice in front of the mirror, in front of a camera or in front of a small audience. Practice, practice, practice. Tony Robbins is Tony Robbins for a reason. You can even hire a speaking coach if necessary (Lear, 2016). You are only going to become better at public speaking with practice and input from others.

Chapter Summary

Public speaking is a skill that many should master but very few do. While it can take a lifetime to truly master everything you need to become a great public speaker, there are certainly things that you can work on now to improve your public speaking skills.

- Don't get too technical with niche phrases that only other experts will understand.
- Make sure to leave your audience with something that will brighten their day.
- Practice, practice, practice!
- Be highly aware of your body language.
- Less is more, don't rely on multimedia to get your points across.
- Be welcoming of constructive criticism and feedback.
- Give your audience a reason to care.
- Use your confident voice.

- Be willing to adjust your style of public speaking based on your audience.

Public speaking is an art and a skill that needs to be honed. If you truly want to become a great public speaker, you need to practice as much as you can and in front of whoever you can.

Final Words

Learning how to effectively communicate in the workplace can be a tricky thing, but if done right it can be incredibly powerful. Effective workplace communication takes place through interpersonal communications which are then broken down into verbal and non-verbal communications. In order to truly be an effective communicator, you need to be cognisant of the differences in individual communication styles and any potential barriers to effective communication.

Barriers to effective communication can include anything from interruptions, inattentive listening, a misinterpretation of body language, gender difference, jumping to conclusions and premature reactions to others. Our brains all respond differently to different stimuli as we process through different emotions. When an employee is experiencing stress in the workplace their brains cannot tell if the stress (threat) is real or perceived. This then reacts with the prefrontal cortex and slows down productivity, processing and reasoning, which makes it very difficult to work.

Effective communication in the workplace helps to create a healthy work environment, removes cultural barriers, increases bottom line profits, lessens conflicts, increases employee engagement and productivity, fosters teamwork, promotes innovation, increases employee retention and boosts overall customer satisfaction.

There are many barriers to effective communication in the workplace. These can include, but are not limited to, gender and/or cultural barriers, tone and body language, your emotions taking over, external and internal noise and so on. It is also very important that you keep a positive mindset while in the workplace. Positivity in the workplace has been tied to every measurable aspect of success, which includes profits, productivity and satisfaction. Both employees and employers can benefit from positivity in the workplace.

Good and effective communication also has the power to truly transform a workplace. Effective communication can result in mitigating conflict, increasing employee engagement, creating better client relationships and a more productive and talented workforce. Keep in mind that about 70% of mistakes in businesses are due to a lack of effective communication (Allen, 2019).

Developing a communication style that includes persuasive communication can really take your communication skills to the next level. Your verbal and non-verbal body language, as well as your facial expressions, can play a very large role in how persuasive and influential you are in the workplace. Learning persuasive communication techniques can benefit you in persuading your team members and your company as a whole to change for the better. You need to ensure that you are sending the correct message to your audience with both your verbal and non verbal communication. While you might experience both formal and informal forms of communication at work, it is beneficial to stick to the more formal forms of communication in the workplace.

There are also many different ways that you can use your body language to communicate to your coworkers; making eye contact, your posture, where and how you place your arms while talking or listening are all ways that you non-verbally communicate with your colleagues. Make sure that you are maintaining eye contact while speaking with people, keeping your posture erect and not crossing your arms in front of you while speaking with someone. Let others know that you are aware of their body language as well and try to encourage them to use positive non-verbal communication.

Non-verbal communication also includes facial

expressions. If your face is always tense, people will perceive you as being unlikable. If your facial expressions are always pleasant and soft, you will be perceived as much more likable.

Some of the keys to becoming a better listener at work are:

- Repeating back to the person what they said in your own words.
- Actually listen to what someone else is saying rather than trying to think of what to say next.
- Listen as though you will have to recall the information later on.
- Maintain eye contact with the person you are speaking with.
- Cut out as much distractions and noise as possible.
- Be prepared to listen.
- Be aware of diversity in the workplace.

Being an effective communicator also means that

you can be persuasive when you need to be. Being persuasive and having an influence in the workplace means being likable, having social proof, being consistent, practicing scarcity, having authority and practicing reciprocity.

In addition, effective workplace communicators are also able to give and receive positive criticism. Don't let people giving you feedback hinder your self-esteem or derail your work. Constructive criticism is meant to help you to grow and become a better employee. You must also learn to give self-critique.

It is inevitable that you will run into difficult situations or difficult people in the workplace. It is how you handle them that makes all the difference. Don't go running off to your boss or human resources right away, try and handle the person or situation on your own in a tactful manner first. If your tactics are unsuccessful, then get leadership involved. This holds true for both coworkers or difficult bosses. Ensure that you are encouraging coworkers to utilize effective communication skills as well.

Being an effective leader is all about having charisma and honing your skills as an effective communicator. Effective and charismatic leaders are able to build a connection with their audience, be trustworthy, show humility and vulnerability, exude confidence and maintain a delicate balance between being too serious and being too easygoing and casual. In order to become a master at communicating, you also must use your distinct voice and portray confidence. Effective leaders are also great at goal setting and are able to get their team on board using S.M.A.R.T. goals.

Some of the most common communication mistakes that can jeopardize all of the effective tactics that you have built up are not paying attention to your non-verbal cues, avoiding conflict, jumping to conclusions, being too close-minded and speaking more than you are listening.

Once you have become aware of the tactics that make communication ineffective, it's time to start harnessing the strategies that will make you an effective communicator. Effective communicators are diplomatic, respect cultural differences, trust in their people, use "I" statements and provide positive feedback to their colleagues and employees.

Lastly, mastering the skill of public speaking can be very advantageous to your career. Many people avoid public speaking out of fear. Here are a few tactics that you can use to master the skill of public speaking:

- Leave out the technical jargon.
- Leave your audience with something to brighten their day.
- Practice!
- Be aware of your body language.
- Don't rely too much on multimedia.

- Give your audience a reason to care.
- Use your confident voice.

With all of these tactics at your disposal, you are sure to become a master at effective communication in the workplace in no time!

Resources

Adams, J. (2019). *5 Ways to Become a Master Communicator - Tap Inspect*. [online] . Available at: https://www.tapinspect.com/5-ways-to-become-a-master-communicator/ [Accessed 23 Jun. 2019].

Allan, L. (2019). *Poor Workplace Communication Costs*. [online] Businessperform.com. Available at: http://www.businessperform.com/workplace-communication/poor-communication-costs.html [Accessed 23 Jun. 2019].

Belonwu, V. (2018). *20 Ways to Communicate Effectively With Your Team - Small Business Trends*. [online] Small Business Trends. Available at: https://smallbiztrends.com/2013/11/20-ways-to-communicate-effectively-in-the-workplace.html [Accessed 24 Jun. 2019].

Bosworth, P. (2019, February 13). The Power of Good Communication in the Workplace | Leadership Choice. Retrieved June 10, 2019, from https://leadershipchoice.com/power-good-communication-workplace/

Chadwick, P. (2014). *How the brain responds to feedback - IEDP*. [online] Iedp.com. Available at: https://www.iedp.com/articles/how-the-brain-responds-to-feedback/ [Accessed 24 Jun. 2019].

Cooley, A. (2019). *10 Ways Employees Can Be More Proactive At Work*. [online] Work It Daily. Available at: https://www.workitdaily.com/be-more-proactive-work [Accessed 23 Jun. 2019].

Dabbah, M. (2018, May 17). 3 Examples of Cultural Differences in the Workplace. [online] redshoemovement.com . Available at: https://redshoemovement.com/examples-of-cultural-differences-in-the-workplace/ [Accessed 9 Jun. 2019].

Daskal, L. (2014). *Communication Mistakes to Avoid at All Costs*. [online] Inc.com. Available at: https://www.inc.com/lolly-daskal/common-communication-mistakes-to-avoid.html [Accessed 24 Jun. 2019].

Daskal, L. (2019). *7 Ways to Be a More Effective Leader - Lolly Daskal | Leadership*. [online] Lolly Daskal. Available at: https://www.lollydaskal.com/leadership/7-ways-to-be-a-more-effective-leader/ [Accessed 23 Jun. 2019].

Daum, K. (2019). *How to Give (and Receive) Positive Criticism*. [online] Inc.com. Available at: https://www.inc.com/kevin-daum/how-to-give-and-recieve-positive-criticism.html [Accessed 24 Jun. 2019].

Dean, J. (2010). *How to Influence People - PsyBlog*. [online] PsyBlog. Available at: https://www.spring.org.uk/2010/07/3-universal-goals-to-influence-people.php [Accessed 26 Jun. 2019].

Dean, J. (2019). *20 Simple Steps to the Perfect Persuasive Message - PsyBlog*. [online] PsyBlog. Available at: https://www.spring.org.uk/2010/12/20-simple-steps-to-the-perfect-persuasive-message.php [Accessed 25 Jun. 2019].

Edberg, H. (2019). *How to Become a Better Listener: 10 Simple Tips.* [online] Positivityblog.com. Available at: https://www.positivityblog.com/better-listener/ [Accessed 25 Jun. 2019].

Effectivecommunicationadvice.com. (2019). *Barriers to Effective Communication.* [online] Available at: http://effectivecommunicationadvice.com/barriers [Accessed 22 Jun. 2019].

Frost, S. (2019). *How Body Language Is Used in the Workplace.* [online] Smallbusiness.chron.com. Available at: https://smallbusiness.chron.com/body-language-used-workplace-11773.html [Accessed 25 Jun. 2019].

Galek, C. (2019). *How to Protect Yourself from People Who Waste Your Time.* [online] Inc.com. Available at: https://www.inc.com/candice-galek/how-to-manage-your-time-stop-others-from-wasting-it.html [Accessed 23 Jun. 2019].

Grace, B. (2018). *How To Ask Questions That Get Results: #5 Hot Tips To 1,000X Your Results.*

[online] Noteworthy - The Journal Blog. Available at: https://blog.usejournal.com/5-ways-to-ask-better-questions-thatll-have-you-solving-problems-smarter-and-faster-af872398fc28?gi=87a0f12c5f2c [Accessed 26 Jun. 2019].

Giang, V. (2012). *17 Tips On Becoming A Charismatic Leader*. [online] Business Insider. Available at: https://www.businessinsider.com/17-things-you-need-to-know-if-you-want-to-be-a-charismatic-leader-2012-1#make-people-feel-like-theyre-the-most-intelligent-impressive-and-fascinating-person-in-the-room-2 [Accessed 23 Jun. 2019].

Giang, V. (2019). *17 Tips On Becoming A Charismatic Leader*. [online] Business Insider. Available at: https://www.businessinsider.com/17-things-you-need-to-know-if-you-want-to-be-a-charismatic-leader-2012-1 [Accessed 23 Jun. 2019].

Gottfried, S. (2018). *https://time.com*. [online] Time. Available at: https://time.com/5321644/body-language-mistakes-work-experts/ [Accessed 25 Jun. 2019].

Heathfield, S. (2019). *Dealing With Difficult People Is a Must for Your Career Success*. [online] The Balance Careers. Available at: https://www.thebalancecareers.com/how-to-deal-with-difficult-people-at-work-1919377 [Accessed 26 Jun. 2019].

Heathfield, S. (2019). *Use These Ideas to Know How to Deal With Your Difficult Boss*. [online] The Balance Careers. Available at: https://www.thebalancecareers.com/how-to-deal-with-difficult-bosses-1917887 [Accessed 23 Jun. 2019].

Jenkins, P. (2018). *How Understanding Body Language Can Help You*. [video] Available at: https://www.youtube.com/watch?v=9aWFOK46eqA [Accessed 28 Jun. 2019].

Jenkins, Dr. P. (2018). *Importance Of Positivity In The Workplace* [YouTube]. Retrieved June 9, 2019, Available at: https://www.youtube.com/watch?v=AbzJNSIJPbk [Accessed 9 Jun 2019].

Kaplan, E. (2016). *How to Become a Master at Public Speaking, According to The Guy Who Runs TED Talks*. [online] Medium. Available at: https://medium.com/the-mission/how-to-become-a-master-at-public-speaking-according-to-the-guy-who-runs-ted-talks-d65433eb057d [Accessed 24 Jun. 2019].

Lear, K. (2019). *How To Become A Master At Public Speaking*. [online] Vunela. Available at: https://vunela.com/how-to-become-a-master-at-public-speaking/ [Accessed 24 Jun. 2019].

Miglani, B., Ivankovich, M., James, R. and Rodarte, C. (2019). *3 Tips on How to Deal With Difficult Work Situations*. [online] Embrace The Chaos. Available at: https://www.embracethechaos.com/2013/11/3-tips-on-how-to-deal-with-difficult-work-situations/ [Accessed 23 Jun. 2019].

Moawad, H. (2017). *How the Brain Processes Emotions*. [online] Neurology Times. Available at: https://www.neurologytimes.com/blog/how-brain-processes-emotions [Accessed 28 Jun. 2019].

Mugavin, B. (2019). *4 Leadership Tips to Inspire a Shared Vision*. [online] Flashpointleadership.com. Available at: https://www.flashpointleadership.com/blog/leadership-tips-inspire-a-shared-vision [Accessed 23 Jun. 2019].

Page, M. (2019). *The importance of good communication in the workplace | Michael Page UK*. [online] Michael Page. Available at: https://www.michaelpage.co.uk/advice/management-advice/development-and-retention/importance-good-communication-workplace [Accessed 25 Jun. 2019].

Peck, D. (2017). *5 Leadership Goal Setting Tips for Making 2018 a Success*. [online] Huffpost.com. Available at: https://www.huffpost.com/entry/5-leadership-goal-setting-tips-for-making-2018-a-success_b_5a26c653e4b0f7f1679a0368 [Accessed 23 Jun. 2019].

Petersen, L. (2019). *The Importance of Good Writing Skills in the Workplace*. [online]

Smallbusiness.chron.com. Available at: https://smallbusiness.chron.com/importance-good-writing-skills-workplace-10931.html [Accessed 26 Jun. 2019].

Redmond, R. (2018). *How to Report Status on a Project*. [online] Project Smart. Available at: https://www.projectsmart.co.uk/how-to-report-status-on-a-project.php [Accessed 26 Jun. 2019].

Richason IV, O. (2017). *What is Effective Workplace Communication?*. [online] Smallbusiness.chron.com. Available at: https://smallbusiness.chron.com/effective-workplace-communication-822.html [Accessed 25 Jun. 2019].

Rosenberg McKay, D. (2018). *Why You Must Identify Your Work Values If You Want Job Satisfaction*. [online] The Balance Careers. Available at: https://www.thebalancecareers.com/identifying-your-work-values-526174 [Accessed 23 Jun. 2019].

Russell, M. (2015). *How your facial expressions at*

work could be hurting your career. [online] Business Insider. Available at: https://www.businessinsider.com/your-facial-expressions-at-work-could-be-hurting-your-career-2015-4?international=true&r=US&IR=T [Accessed 25 Jun. 2019].

S, S. (2018). *Difference Between Verbal and Nonverbal Communication (with Comparison Chart) - Key Differences*. [online] Key Differences. Available at: https://keydifferences.com/difference-between-verbal-and-non-verbal-communication.html [Accessed 25 Jun. 2019].

Scivicque, C. (2010). *How To Find Your Voice At Work*. [online] Forbes.com. Available at: https://www.forbes.com/sites/work-in-progress/2010/11/08/how-to-find-your-voice-at-work/#7f41541430ba [Accessed 23 Jun. 2019].

Scivicque, C. (2018). *How to be Proactive at Work: A Five Step System*. [online] Eat Your Career. Available at: https://eatyourcareer.com/2010/08/how-be-proactive-at-work-step-system/ [Accessed 25 Jun.

2019].

Stachowiak, D. (2019). *6 Habits to Keep People from Wasting Your Time*. [online] Coaching for Leaders. Available at: https://coachingforleaders.com/6-habits-to-keep-people-from-wasting-your-time/ [Accessed 23 Jun. 2019].

Warner, J. (2019). *The Women's Leadership Gap - Center for American Progress*. [online] Center for American Progress. Available at: https://www.americanprogress.org/issues/women/reports/2017/05/21/432758/womens-leadership-gap/ [Accessed 23 Jun. 2019].

Watson, S. (2019). *10 Tips for Effective Workplace Communication*. [online] HowStuffWorks. Available at: https://money.howstuffworks.com/business/starting-a-job/10-tips-for-effective-workplace-communication.htm [Accessed 24 Jun. 2019].

Webb, C. (2017). *What Are the Two Ways of Communication in the Workplace?*. [online] Smallbusiness.chron.com. Available at:

https://smallbusiness.chron.com/two-ways-communication-workplace-10768.html [Accessed 25 Jun. 2019].

Whalen, D. (2018). *13 Powerful Actions Great Leaders Take to Build Great Teams - Medium.* [online] Medium. Available at: https://medium.com/swlh/13-powerful-actions-great-leaders-take-to-build-great-teams-5990c052059f [Accessed 23 Jun. 2019].

Zambas, J. (2019). *The Importance of Effective Communication in the Workplace.* [online] Careeraddict.com. Available at: https://www.careeraddict.com/the-importance-of-effective-communication-in-the-workplace [Accessed 25 Jun. 2019].

Zenbooth (2019). *Solved: How to Stop Loud, Disruptive Coworkers.* [online] Zenbooth. Available at: https://zenbooth.net/blogs/zenbooth-blog/9-tips-for-dealing-with-loud-disruptive-coworkers [Accessed 25 Jun. 2019].

www.ingramcontent.com/pod-product-compliance
Lightning Source LLC
Chambersburg PA
CBHW020244010526
44107CB00002B/88